Women Who Love
Sex Addicts

by Douglas Weiss, LPC, LCDC, LMFT
and Dianne DeBusk, CEAP, CADAC

Discovery Press
Fort Worth, Texas

Contents

PART III—Solutions

Dedicated to the women who have lived so long
with the secret.

Acknowledgments

The authors would like to gratefully acknowledge the contributions of all the women who shared their stories, their lives, their pain and recovery with us. We thank you. Without your honesty, courage and willingness to share, this book would not have been possible. You and your stories exemplify the experience, strength and hope so often referred to in recovery programs. It is our hope that together our words and yours will reach into the hearts of women everywhere who read these pages, and offer them hope for their own growth and recovery from the painful reality of living with and loving a sex addict.

Introduction

Over the past half century, doctors, clergy and therapists have helped their patients identify and recover from many addictive disorders, including alcoholism, drug addiction, compulsive overeating, compulsive gambling, co-dependency and workaholism. Many more individuals have identified these issues in their own lives. In addition to recognizing these problems, American culture in the 1990's has moved on to identify sexual addiction. In recent years much has been written about sexual addiction, and today many sexual addicts are getting effective treatment and entering programs of recovery.

A person's alcoholism or drug addiction creates what has come to be known as a co-dependent response in family members and others who love the addict. The same is true of sexual addiction. It is the purpose of this book to discuss the nature of this response, what we call sexual co-dependency. While not all sexual co-dependents are women, the majority are, and it is these women who love sex addicts whom we are attempting to reach with this book. However, it is our hope that anyone in a process of recovery from any addictive disorder will find the material contained in this text of value.

We have dug deeply into ourselves and into our own experiences, as well as those of others who have suffered from this particular affliction, in an effort to assist individuals in their search to become more healthy and whole. It is our fervent hope that our efforts will enhance the overall well-being of our American culture.

Sexual Addiction

There are many fine books available that define and discuss the sexual addict. For our purposes here, a general definition will suffice. Basically, a sexual addict is someone who, due to childhood sexual abuse, inordinate exposure to sexual material, or sexual interactions as a child, develops sexual behaviors that allow him or her to escape, momentarily, from intense feelings of shame and unworthiness. These behaviors can range from compulsive masturbation to cross dressing to compulsive sexual acting out in heterosexual or homosexual relationships. Some behaviors exhibited by sexual addicts are "socially acceptable". Some are not. Some are even illegal. The range of behaviors is wide, and the consequences of the behaviors varies from person to person and situation to situation.

Perhaps you have identified for the first time that the man you love has a sexual addiction. Maybe you already knew it before you picked up this book. Or, you may still be unsure. Generally speaking, if the sexual behavior of your partner and your responses to it concern you, you need to keep reading.

Co-Dependency and Sexual Co-Dependency

Co-dependency can be defined as compulsive use of a set of maladaptive, often counterproductive behaviors (behaviors that don't work) in an attempt to create a sense of identity, value or safety in one's life. Co-dependents seek validation and meaning for their lives in the world of people, places and things outside themselves. They believe that other people's behavior or treatment of them in some way adds to or detracts from their

10

own value. Through various behaviors such as rationalization, minimization, efforts to control, manipulation and denial, they create the illusion, even to themselves, that they are okay because the people and things around them are arranged just right. They can go to great, even life-threatening lengths to preserve this false sense of identity, value and safety.

Sexual co-dependency includes the additional dimension of a distorted sense of the sexual self, an inability of these co-dependents to separate their value from their sexuality. In a relationship with a sex addict, whether it is as a child being sexually abused, or as the adult partner of a sex addict, the woman who loves the addict is the human being the addict is using to feed his addiction. She becomes an object to him instead of a person. This is always damaging to self esteem, but if this happens before the age where she has developed some sense of individual identity or self, she will consistently have trouble seeing herself as having any value at all independent of her ability to feed his addiction and in some magical way make him okay. She will feel incomplete without a man there to "objectify" her. If she was abused as a child, she may feel unsafe much of the time, and use her sexuality as well as other behaviors (such as denial, people pleasing, perfectionism) to keep a man in her life to "protect" her from other potential abusers. Ironically, her low self esteem will prevent her from believing that she is worthy of being kept safe or treated well, and she will frequently choose abusive, controlling men as her "protectors".

In the following chapters, you will find the stories of some women who love and have loved sexual addicts, written in their own words. The stories are followed by an in-depth discussion of the similarities these women share. The last section of the book is dedicated to recovery from sexual co-dependency. There is hope for all women who love sex addicts, whether the addict gets help or not.

Part I—Our Stories

1

Me and My Addict

(Authors' note: The following story was written by a woman we'll call Monica. Monica is married to a recovering sex addict, and has three children. She has been involved in therapy and recovery groups for nearly two years.)

If I'd only known then what I know now. There was something "familiar" about John. He didn't appear to be at all like anyone in my family, but as it turned out, he was a friendly version of my mom, whom I had many unresolved issues with. I believed only the best about him. Even when an old friend of his, as well as his dad questioned me about whether I really knew what I was getting into, I just smiled my, "look smart on the outside, though brainless on the inside," smile and said, "Of course I do." Well, I was wrong. It was like I had found a man who would marry me, and let me live in my Cinderella fantasy, even though he didn't come close to being any of it, in reality. I even looked at the way his dad cleared the table for his mom, and though John had never evidenced that kind of thoughtfulness, I reasoned in my heart, "Well if that's his dad, surely John's got some of that in him."

From the honeymoon on, our sexual encounters were disappointing. I knew what I wanted to have happen, but coming from my "no talk" background, I had no way to convey it. So, I reasoned, I must not be very enjoyable to my husband. In dating he had seemed so noble in not engaging in petting. What puzzled me was that he didn't engage in it afterward either. He didn't seem interested in arousing me sexually but was quite thorough in training me in what I should do for him. I should have woke up to something not being right when he finally told me to fantasize to get excited. But since I seemed locked in a gullible world, I just went along with it, and he had me convinced that this was the way everyone's marriage was. They just didn't talk about this part.

Now, I'd grown up in a family where you never admit you're wrong or have made a mistake. Rather, somehow, you become "superwoman or man" and overcome the obstacles, do more to compensate for shortcomings, no matter whose they are. I was teaching school, doing the housework, fixing the meals, while my husband was working on his Master's degree. But what I saw was my husband spending his time when I got home, watching TV and spending great amounts of money and time on video games. I did resent him for it, but I always reasoned that I must be wrong. This is what marriage is supposed to be, right? I've just got to work harder so he'll be more pleased with me than the TV. Of course, that never worked.

My husband and I have had some pleasant times together. I do feel like I married my best friend, and I am sure that God wanted me to marry him. Perhaps, that's been my only essence of hope for our relationship. If God okayed it, surely he has a purpose.

John and I lived in a state of emotional survival our first ten years. And as it is with addiction, you either get better or worse. He got worse. And I came to the point in my practice of fantasizing and masturbating that I finally said, "It may not be wrong for him, but between me and God, I think this is wrong. I don't want to do this anymore." So I didn't. It was a fight, but the more victories I had, the more I knew I couldn't afford to give in to it again.

After the birth of our third child, I was feeling desperate. My husband seemed like a fourth child living in our home; mad at me for giving attention to the children and not having enough sex with him. It was the first time I remember being able to ask him to behave in a different way because I had a need. I believe he gave it a try, but he seemed enslaved to the habits he'd been practicing. My greatest horror occurred when he started telling me about the inappropriate ways he was treating our third child—still an infant—behind my back. I'd wondered why she looked so traumatized after he baby sat her. Well, if pain is the thing that leads to change, I'd hit my quota. "God," I cried, "What do you want from me?"

"Grow up!" was the answer. And I had no idea how retarded I was. My husband did go into some sexual addiction recovery and I started the co-dependent journey.

For me, breaking all my erroneous beliefs has been like dropping the tablets Moses brought from God. I thought I was perfect, but I was human. I thought I was truthful, but I had even defrauded myself. The worst part of co-dependency for me was that my worth was established by my "drug"—my mother first, my husband next—by their behavior toward me. And they didn't have nice behavior toward me. Now all of God's behavior toward me has been truthful, loving, genuine, dependable, merciful and with eternal purpose. I've just begun, finally, to "grow up"!

2

Julie's Story

My name is Julie. I'm a woman who loves sex addicts. It took me a long time to be able to say those words. Even when I started saying them in support group meetings, I didn't really understand or believe how true they are for me. If anyone had told me back then that I'd be putting those words and my story down on paper, I would have said to myself, "All but the parts that would make me look bad. And maybe some of those other things that happened would be too shocking to really tell anyone. If people really knew me, they wouldn't like me. I couldn't possibly tell that . . ."

Today I know some things about life and about me that I didn't know back then. I know that there is no hurt so bad that love cannot heal it. I know that I am, and always have been, precious and perfect in the eyes of my God. I know that, given the family I was born into and their particular set of beliefs and behaviors, there was never a chance that I would make healthy choices as an adult. For me to choose a man who was not a sex addict would have been unnatural. I'm always amazed and a little skeptical that some women with histories similar to mine grew up and married men who were not sex addicts. Where did they learn to do that?

I was born in the early 1950's, the second daughter of a couple who would later have two sons. I grew up in the suburbs. My parents probably looked pretty typical for that period: my mother stayed at home with us kids, Dad finished college and became a schoolteacher. We had three meals a day, went to school, did homework and helped around the house. We fought and played and took vacations. We had pets and lots of neighborhood friends. If you didn't look too far beneath the surface my family made a pretty picture. But it was the part of the picture you couldn't see that created the person I became: due to constant childhood sexual abuse, I became a little girl walking around in an adult body, afraid that any moment I would again be sexually assaulted.

I wasn't allowed to date much in high school. My mother had rigid rules about curfew, make-up, the kind of movies I could see, the clothes I could wear. I reached adulthood believing that I should be a virgin when I married, and that I should always be married to the same man. I planned to marry my high school sweetheart, and turned down a nursing scholarship so I could stay near him. I got a job, started nurses' training at the local community college and started creating what I thought would be a pretty picture of my own. Then I married a sex addict.

I didn't know Jack was a sex addict. We met when my boyfriend decided he wanted to date other girls. Jack was older and knew a whole lot about life that I didn't know. He had friends who drank and smoked pot, although he didn't. He came from a divorced family and had had an unhappy childhood. He knew I was the right girl for him because I was so wholesome looking, and could cook and clean house and take good care of him. He needed someone to make him happy. He was 25. I was a naive 19 year old who looked much younger and acted much older. He wanted me to move in with him, and I was afraid to tell my parents we were living together, so I married him.

My parents were appalled. They didn't like Jack, but finally agreed to participate in our wedding. A few days before the wedding, my dad played a special song on the stereo for me: "I'm Just a Girl Who Can't Say No" from the musical *Oklahoma*. At the time, I didn't understand what he meant. And I didn't understand till much later that I was a girl who couldn't say no to a man, or that I learned it from being sexually abused for most of my childhood by both of my grandfathers and an uncle.

A few months into my marriage, Jack got a job working in a pornography shop. He didn't drive, so I would leave the house after working the evening shift at the local hospital and drive downtown to pick him up when he got off work at 2 a.m. I had never been exposed to pornography, other than the occasional *Playboy Magazine* when I was growing up. I had never been to "that part of town" before. I had no idea that I was endangering myself. I thought it was my duty as a wife to provide whatever my husband needed. Mother had always done so many kind little things for Dad, it seemed natural.

I had been sexual with my high school sweetheart, but Jack exposed me to the seamier side of sex. I was a little unsure of most of it, but he assured me I had just led a sheltered life, and that everyone lived this way. He convinced me that this was love, and that my family didn't know anything about love. I was trained to give all my power to a man who was being sexual with me. It was ingrained in me from years of sexual abuse. I believed Jack was right. I was afraid to disagree with him. And I didn't want anybody to see beneath the surface of my pretty picture.

The problem was, the picture was getting uglier and uglier. Jack had sex with the teenage girls who were his little sisters' friends. When he told me about it the first time, I didn't confront him, I yelled at the 14 year old girls. He had sex with his brother's wife. Once again I blamed the woman. He sent two young men out to our house one night to have sex with me while he was at work. I didn't say no. He had sex with prostitutes, claiming that he wasn't getting enough from me because I was pregnant. I drew the line when he wanted me to "swap" with a couple he met at his store. He'd gone into the back room at work to have sex with the husband.

After the birth of our daughter, I began to withdraw sexually from him. Our daughter had severe medical problems that required a lot of time and attention. Jack began to spend more time watching dirty movies and masturbating. He stopped telling me about his sexual exploits, and I didn't ask. He brought home books from his store about uncles and nieces and fathers and daughters. I felt uncomfortable enough about that to tell him he'd better never think about doing anything sexual with our daughter. But I didn't leave him. That would ruin the picture.

I went back to work. I thought it would fill the growing emptiness in me, brought about by my unwillingness to be close to a man as depraved as I thought my husband was. I hated what he was doing, but still felt rejected. I had a brief affair with a family friend whose wife had died, but I was consumed with guilt.

I took one job, then had to leave after four months because one of the men who supervised me propositioned me, and I couldn't say no. Quitting was the only way I knew to take care of the situation. I instinctively knew I wouldn't be able to withstand further advances from him, although I desperately wanted to.

I took another job working in a hospital. I excelled at my work, as I had excelled in school, and began to gain a little self esteem.

I developed friendships and made some positive changes for myself. I opened a checking account (something Jack would never allow me to do before). I began to live a split life. At work I was capable and mature. At home I was withdrawn and depressed. As Jack resorted to more and more ritualized masturbation, often staying up all night, I felt more and more rejected. He preferred his movies and books to me. I wanted closeness and affection but felt guilty being unfaithful.

He had repeatedly told me he would destroy me emotionally if I ever divorced him, and that he would take our daughter where I could never find her. I couldn't see a way out, and in despair one night, with a bottle of muscle relaxers in my hand, I called the suicide hotline.

I don't know if I would have killed myself or not, but that call put me in touch with a counselor and, while I never told him the whole story, I did develop the courage to leave Jack and file for divorce.

It remained a struggle for me to set boundaries with him, and there were times during the process of separation and divorce that I considered returning to the marriage. I was still a little girl in a woman's body, and frightened of being alone in a world of men. I didn't know what was wrong with me, I just knew if a man wanted something from me, I felt compelled to give it to him. I had no sense of a right to my own body; if a man expressed an interest in me sexually, I had no choice but to give him what he wanted. Of course, I usually hated myself afterwards. Staying married to a sexual abuser seemed preferable to being alone in a world where I couldn't protect myself.

Somehow, I found the strength to go through with the divorce. I dated a little, and always had the same trouble saying no and setting sexual boundaries. Because of our daughter's illness, I still had to have contact with my ex-husband and, although we were no longer sexual, he still had the ability to frighten me and took every opportunity to do so. In a desperate attempt to end his emotional dominance over me I decided to move out of state. I sold my home and moved.

In Twelve Step programs they call a move like mine a "geographical cure." I thought if I moved, my problems would disappear. I thought the sex addict was my problem, and that if I put 2,000 miles between us, I would somehow magically be okay.

Of course, I took me with me, and nothing really changed. I was still frightened and insecure. I still subconsciously (or perhaps semi-consciously) knew that I would not be able to set boundaries with men. So I did the only thing I knew that would protect me: I got married again. This time, the man I chose was not only a sex addict, he was a practicing alcoholic. Once again, I made a decision based on fear. The results were frighteningly similar. I assumed the caretaker role, giving a semblance of normalcy to the life of a man whose actions were out of control. I had another child, trying to recreate my pretty picture. For awhile, it worked.

As Bill's drinking increased, I tried all the usual methods of control. I mixed his drinks so they wouldn't be so strong. I made special dinners in an effort to get him to come home. I cooked and cleaned and kept both children quiet when he had a hangover.

It wasn't until he started having affairs and staying gone for days at a time that I truly began to feel rejected. Once again, I wasn't good enough to keep a man in my life.

I decided that I'd been too nice, and that maybe complaining was the answer. The more I complained, the more he drank and slept around. He was gone more than ever, and my behavior became more and more out of control. Once again, I contemplated suicide. I felt that anyone other than myself could do a better job of maintaining a family. At my lowest moment, I even considered sending my daughter to live with her father. I felt that a practicing sex addict with an affinity for teenage girls would be a better parent than I was.

Thank God it was not long before someone told me about Al-Anon. I began attending meetings, looking for a way to get Bill to stop drinking, so he would stay home with us. We separated, reunited (it was Christmas, after all), and separated a final time. He went to treatment, but did not stay sober, and never stopped having affairs. I started seeing a man I met at my meetings, and eventually Bill and I divorced.

I began to work on a program of recovery for myself, got a job, and made changes in many areas of my life. I continued to date the man I'd met who was a recovering alcoholic, and we lived together for a year. I don't know if I loved Jimmy, or was just afraid of being alone. If I hadn't met him, I would have met someone else and probably repeated the same pattern. After a year though, I knew I was unhappy in that relationship. I couldn't say no when he wanted sex, even when I didn't, and I participated in some sexual activities I was uncomfortable with. I thought I would be better off alone.

I'm sure my life for the next few years looked out of control to the people who cared about me. If I dated a man and he told me he cared about me, I would convince myself I was in love with him. It was the only way I could justify, in my mind, the fact that I was sexual with him. It was okay if we were in love, I told myself. But deep down, I felt more shame with each new relationship.

I continued to work on my recovery in the Al-Anon program, went back to school, and made strides in my career. I was never out of a relationship for more than a few weeks. I began to have more memories of my childhood sexual abuse. I spent a year in a group therapy for women who were incest survivors. I was as honest as I could be, but never really let my barriers down. It was pointed out to me that perhaps I might want to spend six months or so not in any relationship at all, and I really intended to do that every time one ended, but it never happened. I still didn't know I could say no to a man, and I still had to convince myself I was in love with each one after we had sex. Most of them were not interested in me as a person, and none of them gave me what I really wanted, which was permission to say no to them.

It took another two years and a lot of emotional, spiritual, physical and financial pain to bring me to "my bottom". I suffered through the end of a relationship with a married man who I was sure I loved very much. Within two weeks of the end of that relationship, I accepted a date with a man I worked with, and, even though I knew from the first moment that I didn't want to be with this man, I couldn't say no.

Of course I had to "fall in love" with him, and begin to take financial, physical, and emotional care of him. That's what good women do. In this case, though, it nearly killed me. This man was another sex addict, and unbeknownst even to himself, was a carrier of hepatitis B.

The fourteen months that I was involved with Charlie were the most costly of my life. I had just recovered from a hysterectomy and had had the courage to break up with him when I had the first symptoms of hepatitis. I quickly became very ill, and he offered to help, so I let him back into my life. Even when I found out I'd been infected by him, I let him stay. I became sicker and sicker, but still did not say no to him sexually. I barely had the energy to get out of bed, but in one weekend we had sex four times.

A few days later, I was hospitalized. While I was in the hospital, I developed a perineal rash that the doctor thought was herpes. When I told Charlie, he admitted that his ex-wife had had herpes, but denied that he had ever had it. I was devastated, and for a day or so until the lab reports came back, I was overcome with shame for how my life was turning out. Thank God the lab reports showed that it was not herpes, and after twelve days in the hospital I went home.

I was still very ill, and lost four months at work. My children and I lived on food stamps, financial help from my church, and a loan from my parents. My friends at work helped me with money and groceries. And still, I did not break up with Charlie. In the insanity of my disease, we moved in together. It only took another four months for me to see that Charlie's sexual addiction was out of control, and that his anger was affecting my children. I began to attend Co-SA meetings (meetings for people who love someone who is a sex addict), and finally found the courage to ask him to leave.

Over the next few months, I dated some, but was able to set some sexual boundaries. I began to identify some of my dysfunctional sexual behaviors. I was serious about changing myself so I would not have to continue to give my power away to sex addicts. It became very clear that I needed to have some intense therapy about my childhood sexual abuse issues, and I entered a psychiatric hospital to do just that.

As a result of that month in treatment, I was able to identify the origins of many of my adult behaviors. It was an extremely painful experience, as I retrieved memories of abuse that started when I was a baby. I could see how there was never any question about my being able to say no to a man when he wanted something from me. I was able to give back most of the shame that kept me locked into my behavior patterns to the perpetrators from my childhood (there were three), and to the people who didn't protect me.

I discovered that I had lived my adult life from the perspective of that abused child: I needed someone to protect me from the abusers that could come along any moment. And I went to great lengths to keep a man in my life to do just that.

It's been two years since I was in treatment. I continue to work on my recovery program on a daily basis. Today I know that, while I could not protect myself as a child, I can now. I am able to recognize abusive behavior, and take steps to keep myself safe. I can say no to advances from a man a long time before they become sexual. I am more in touch with my reality, and know when someone tries to deny my sense of what is real. I have discovered the precious innocent child that I was before the abuse started, and am able to hear her when she tells me something. She was always there, trying to communicate with me, but I had a long history of not listening to her when she told me something was wrong. I had taught myself a long time ago to ignore that child, and she still has a hard time trusting me. I have learned though, that I must be trustworthy to myself before I will attract trustworthy people into my life. Thank God I am learning to act in my own best interest.

Recovery for me has not always been smooth. There are times when I am tempted to return to old behaviors. There are times when my injured inner child feels extremely unsafe and tries to convince me that only a man can provide the safety I seek. Today the adult in me knows that this is a lie, and I choose to make my choices from my adult perspective. When I spend any amount of time around a sex addict I begin to feel frightened. I can still give up my reality to a sex addict if I'm not careful. I process my thoughts, feelings, and actions on a daily basis with the women in my support group, and rely heavily on a higher power, so I continue to grow.

Sexual co-dependency has been referred to as a disease with effects as devastating as sexual addiction. I know this to be true for me. My story confirms it. I could have died from my disease, and no sex addict would ever have stopped me. Thankfully, my recovery does not depend on anyone but me. Today, I am in charge of creating my own picture. And while it may not always be a "pretty" picture, it will at least be an honest one.

3

Learning To Be Me

Hi! My name is Carla. I am a woman who has loved a sex addict. I'm co-dependent to sex addicts. Well, actually I am co-dependent to anything that eats, sleeps, and breathes. Maybe even a few things that don't eat, sleep and breathe. Life is okay today, but let me tell you, it still has its moments. A year ago I wouldn't have told you that I thought life was great and that just being alive was a blessing. Today, at least 80% of the time I can tell you those things and mean them. The other 20% of the time, well . . . I call that time my "period of preparation for gratitude!!" Well, here goes . . .

I am writing my story more for me than for you. Although I do hope that you read my story, and perhaps know that at the very least you are not alone. I have felt different or alone more or less for the last fifteen years. I don't remember feelings of extreme loneliness or being different in my early childhood. However, from the time of being very small, I do remember feeling that if I could make people laugh, smile, think I was great, then life seemed so much better.

I especially remember these feelings in response to being with my grandmother. She loved me deeply, but I was her star. I was going to live out everything that she had not been able to do. I remember being told how smart I was, and that I could accomplish everything that I set out to do. My parents were very supportive of the things that I wanted to try, and the decisions that I made. However, (and here is the kicker) life in a "baggie" does not allow a kid any preparation for what is going to be waiting for them. I had no coping skills for certain situations. I thought that if I wanted something, I got it. I thought that if I wanted something to work out, it did.

I was popular in high school. I was a cheerleader. I received Scholastic honors. I was a high achiever. Are you surprised? I didn't think that you would be. Everything had always been so easy, it seemed.

When I went to Europe my senior year in high school, I was like a fish out of water. It was the first time I had been away from my family for an extended period of time. Part of me wanted to go home, and the other part wanted to stay and see the sights. I remember feeling naked without my family. I didn't feel as "old" as the other kids. I didn't do the things they did, and I would sometimes feel left out. But, at least I didn't do those things they did "just to belong." Still, it seemed awfully lonely sometimes. I didn't feel good about myself for not doing those things. I wasn't proud at those times that I had my "own path." In fact, I thought having my own path was more a form of persecution instead of a statement of personal faith and integrity.

In my family, people get married, and they stay virgins until they get married. I don't remember thinking about sex very much as a student in high school. I remember being more interested in horses and dogs. I had a boyfriend all the way through high school. He was wonderful. That is probably why I broke up with him.

A week after I came back from Europe, I met my first husband. He was crazy and I loved him on sight. How "UNBORING" he was. We were together for three years before we got married. On the night before we got married, I knew that

I didn't want to get married. But how could I disappoint all those people? Especially my grandmother. She loved him. She was crazy about him. She would die if the wedding didn't go on as planned.

Now I tell you these were my own perceptions of the situation. My parents didn't want me to marry him. They said we could freeze all of the food. No problem. Don't do it if you don't want to. And, in my mind, I am thinking, "Yeah, sure." But it was my decision. I was powerless to do anything else. He was mine. I decided to get married.

I worked full time and went to school full time. In the midst of all that, I was living in verbal, spiritual, and emotional abuse. "You're ugly. Spoiled brat. Mama's baby. Lazy. No fun." You name it, he said it. He also began to drink. He was not fun when he drank. He got physically sick.

After two years, I left. I knew somehow that I was not all of those things that he called me. But really I think that I somehow believed them. The reason I left was because I was just plain tired of the pain. It was that simple. I don't think that I consciously wanted to save myself. For a kid who grew up in a security blanket, this situation was nuts. But even recognizing it was crazy, I dated my first husband for a year after our separation and during the divorce.

Oh, and by the way, I was still sucking my thumb at the age of twenty-three. Literally.

The abuse of my first husband—which I thought was really no big deal and, in fact, did not recognize as abuse until years later—helped to set a pattern of my taking on responsibility for everything that went wrong. I was always willing to take the blame, but never the triumph. Someone else was always responsible for the good stuff.

I met my second husband, an old friend from high school, a month after my divorce was final. After being a victim in my first marriage, I was going to take a hostage in my second. And that's what I did.

My second husband was a nice guy, and he went along with anything that I wanted. While we were dating, I found out that I was pregnant. I thought immediately of my family, and knew that I couldn't have the baby. I had an abortion.

We were married two months later. Two months after that, I was pregnant again, and later had a son.

Not too long after I got married, I knew that I had made another mistake. I felt dumb and stupid. A person who has never before known what failure was does not cope very well with failure staring her in the face. I couldn't stand it that I had messed up my life so badly in the last nine years. I felt that the only things I had done well were the birth of my son and my professional career as an accountant.

My physical health began to deteriorate. I had frequent migraine headaches. It didn't take me long to figure out that medication could help me cope with more than just physical pain. It dulled the physical pain, and helped me escape the much more excruciating emotional pain. Pretty soon, I couldn't differentiate between the two. Prescription drugs became a very big part of my life.

My out-of-control behavior with drugs did not last very long. But let me tell you, the losses were great. Although I do believe that my co-dependency led me into drug addiction, I was unteachable as long as my mind was chemically affected.

My parents did an intervention, and I went to treatment. That was in 1986. I left my second husband. I never came home to him from the hospital.

I started going to Twelve Step meetings. It was there that I met my third husband. He was a heroin addict who had been struggling in and out of the program for years. Of course, I hooked up with him. What better way to belong, and take the focus off of me? I didn't know it then, but my husband was also an out-of-control sex addict. He acted out all the five years of our relationship, even after the birth of my next two children.

Throughout the relationship, I confronted his behavior. He always had an alibi, or a ready excuse. He was good. He was also my God, my higher power. I believed him. I guess I wanted to. The shame at having another marriage not work would have been too much for me to bear. I stayed.

None of our friends wanted to break my husband's secrets. I knew that something was terribly wrong. So I called one of our friends, and told him that I already knew, and would he help me intervene. After the secret was broken, the help came. My husband did not want to go to treatment. He didn't want to leave his business. However, a month later, his partner told him he had to go. He went.

I remember feeling angry and helpless at the same time. How stupid was I, not to have known what was going on? The intellectual shame was overwhelming.

I went out to his treatment center for family week. I had a lot of medical testing—including an AIDS test. I had two sexually transmitted diseases. I became scared to death that I would have AIDS, too. I almost came apart. While at the doctor for all of the bad news, I asked for something for my nerves. I got it. It helped me to not come apart. It also led me to be intervened on, and go to co-dependency treatment myself.

Even after treatment, my husband's acting out didn't stop. He told me that the day I got home from treatment. On the day after I completed treatment, we separated. He had been seeing someone while I was gone, and continued to see her for a while.

At this point, all I could think of is how I was now the mother of three children. I was in a relationship with someone who did not want the same things I did. But, I had to own that although my path had been laid for me long before I began to actively make my own choices, only I was responsible for being in this situation. No one else. It was not my fault that my husband was a sex addict. But, it was my co-dependency that put me in his orbit to be hurt. As long as I didn't look at my issues I knew that I would make the same mistake again.

We had been separated six months when our divorce was final. The more I learned about my husband's sexual addiction, the more scared I became. The risk was too great for me. I know that recovery for couples from sexual addiction happens. Our relationship had more wrong with it than sexual addiction. When I am out of his insanity, my own insanity becomes apparent very quickly. I have to work on me first.

We tried for six months before we separated. The pain was too great for us to overcome as a couple. Even though we had had children together, the very substance of the marriage was not strong enough to support the struggling that we each had to go through individually.

I want you to understand that I gave little pieces of myself away over the last fifteen years. I emotionally prostituted myself. The pain through all of this was great. I cannot describe to you the mountain-loads of shame and guilt. At times of clarity, I knew that I was lovable. But somehow I didn't have the tools to break all of the cycles.

Through my years in recovery in another Twelve Step program, some things began to change. One of those things was the realization that I used my husband's disease to my own end. This is part of my co-sexual addiction. I wanted a relationship. What better person to have one with than a sex addict whose attention is elsewhere? I didn't have the skills to make a relationship work. I picked someone not only without those skills, but someone who would give what I wanted without asking too much in return. In recovery, however, I started to want more. I started to wake up. Coming out of the fog was like having surgery without anesthetic. It was a painful process.

Today, I struggle. But life is so good. Just last night I had a shame and panic attack that felt like Pearl Harbor. But you know what? The roller coaster ride is a lot more level today than it was a year ago. I just celebrated a year in a recovery program for women who love sex addicts (Co-SA). Today I am exploring so many things. I am scraping my knees, struggling with who I am and what I am about. The only thing I do know today is that I want to strive for wellness and okayness. I believe the name for that is serenity.

Like any other compulsive and obsessive behavior disorder, co-dependency is progressive. My co-dependency progressed from a problem drinker, to an alcoholic, to an addict, alcoholic and sex addict. I have to know this. If I don't learn about my own behavior, who will it be next time? That thought just about scares me to death.

I am told that the grief process will take anywhere from two to seven years. OH GOD!!!!!!! Life can be so hard! I do grieve today, along with the wailing and gnashing of teeth.

Through all this, my kids have been wonderful, even though all of this change has not been easy for them. I have three children now. They are very outspoken, almost militant. But, I am letting them feel their power. Their personal power will help them in their struggle for high self-regard and self-love. I want that for them.

My children's father and I are in recovery today. He has his own path, I have mine. We don't like each other's paths very often. I just try to not have a panic attack when I am not pleasing him or everyone else.

My story is not one of sexual promiscuity. It is a story of personal abandonment. All of us as co-sex addicts are not carbon copies of each other. We are us. Our characteristics do not have to be set in stone for each of us to belong. Recovery is there for those of us who want it. If you are reading our stories I hope you feel hope. You deserve hope. You are precious.

There are a lot of things about me that I like. But there are a lot of things that can still cause me to feel shame. I am a thirty-three year old mother of three kids that has been married three times. Who would want to be with me? I know who. GOD! And ME!

4

Becky's Story

Women who love sex addicts—what a concept. I think for me it is more women who use sex addicts for a fix.

Hi, I am Becky, and I am a woman who loves and is attracted to sex addicts. I did not start out loving sex addicts. In fact I did not want to be near any human being. I was severely depressed and suicidal. I was isolated for a period of five years, hating myself, hating this world and being very angry at the God who made me live through it.

Then one day, when I was sixteen, an obnoxious, perverted, persistent sex addict entered my life. He decided I was the girl for him and proceeded to pester me into going out with him. I had known his reputation as a two-timer and even as a Peeping Tom. The one thing this guy had going for him was he could make me laugh. And in laughing I felt alive.

He loved to go out and party. Through him I learned to drink and entertain. I became able to function in the real world and I no longer hated living. As I got to know him, I realized under that obnoxious exterior was a gentle, kindhearted human being. I knew I did not want to live with this man forever, but I just did not want to leave today.

He started pestering me to get married when I was seventeen, not long after we started having sex. I immediately got pregnant. I knew I did not want to get married. I wanted to go to college and have a career, so I did not tell him that I was pregnant. I was afraid he would force me to marry him; I was afraid I would commit suicide, so I got an abortion. I felt in my heart this child was a girl and even then I was afraid he would abuse her. With these feelings, I still continued to date him.

I began to realize that he was seeing other girls. I felt confused. I did not want to marry him but I still wanted him to date only me, no one else. I never got any "proof". I never was told (that I remember) that someone saw him out with another girl; I never (that I remember) found any item to confront him with. So I let my reality be distorted to his, believing that this was not happening, that my instincts were wrong. When his behavior was too overwhelming, I told myself that I did not care, that this did not hurt me because I was who he continued to see openly. I became part of a triangle to a silent third person.

I did try a few times to get away from him. During one six month stretch a girlfriend literally babysat me day and night to keep me from going back, but after awhile I would always go back. Things on the surface would look great—lots of parties, laughter—but on the inside I knew I had betrayed myself again.

My dad had made an arrangement with me so I could go away to college my last two years. Dad asked me about it one time when we were broken up. I decided to go for it, filled out all the papers, and sent the money before we got back together. Somehow I managed to get off to school, and I loved it. One of my addictions is working, and I threw myself into my studies during the week and then drove home and partied all weekend, then drove back to school. I liked the two worlds being separate. I seldom drank or did drugs during the week but I stayed under the influence of chemicals on the weekends. All this time he had been talking about getting married.

When my degree was completed I had run out of excuses. We were married, bought a house, and I started to work. The "should" was, I was to be a happy bride, but the reality was, I did not want to leave school and I did not want to get married.

I worked with a great group of party people. Soon I was drinking every day, and doing drugs whenever they were around. I felt more fake and more isolated. I was told I had the American dream and I felt numb and depressed.

During this time we went to a counselor because, "I was having trouble adjusting to my new life." While we were seeing her, he was caught red-handed at peeping. He made excuses and the counselor believed him, telling me to go home and make my husband happy and all my troubles would go away.

Somewhere in there I numbed out completely. I threw myself into my work and partied. I emotionally separated myself from him, saying I needed the space. In doing that, I gave him all the space he needed to do whatever it was he did. I never asked questions, and I never tried to find him when he was out of pocket. Our sexual encounters became very few and far between. Sex only brought back home how separate we were, how much I was hurt by his lovers, and how I felt like an object while we had sex. The loneliness was overwhelming, but I did not leave.

Then events took a turn. I found out I was pregnant, and I was terrified. I knew I did not want to grow old with this man but I could not justify another abortion. We decided over drinks that we would have this child and I said I wanted two children, implying we would stay together long enough to have the second child. Because my job was so over-demanding in time and energy—perfect for a workaholic—I had to quit. When my son was five or six weeks old, I was breast feeding him in his bedroom. His father came in wearing his usual (no clothing) and started a conversation. When I looked up I realized he was jacking off, staring at me and the child. My blood went cold. I had thought a son would be safe . . . I immediately got pregnant again and found a job.

Events took another turn; he was transferred out of town a month before our second child was born. Somehow I had enough sense on board to tell him I was not going with him. We owned the house, I was working at a good job, and he would probably be transferred back in a few years. It made sense at the time. This is what I call my year for the crazies. I did not want him near the kids, yet I knew he loved them dearly. I did not want to live with him, yet I talked on the phone to him every day.

There is something terrifying in bringing a daughter home into a sex addicted household. On an unconscious level I had to pick between loving my daughter, or continuing to have a relationship with this man. It hurts to admit that I chose the relationship. I cannot remember anything about my daughter's first year. I can see pictures of her and only know who she is because people have told me.

During this time I picked up a coping skill from my mother: I would eat large amounts of sugar and drink large amounts of caffeine and forget about eating meals unless it was convenient. This combination in my body works a lot like speed. I had energy to take care of the kids, get to work, and keep up a co-addictive relationship with my sex addict husband on the weekends. I developed an ulcer and lost weight. I could literally bounce off the walls.

One day I was given a stress test. For one score, there was a 50% chance of developing a fatal illness, for another an 80%

chance. I had twice the score needed for the 80% chance. I sat myself down, patted myself on the back that I was still alive and then started taking drastic measures to relieve some of the stress. I called my husband. While I was crying I said I did not care what it took, we needed to come live with him.

One of the roles I had played over the years was the "broken angel". By not complaining and being good natured about his friends and partying, I left him with very little to blame me for. I did not shame him about going to strip clubs, I did not inquire about his girlfriends, and I did not complain about the amount of money he spent on pornography. I was truly the "good old girl." My payoff in this was when I asked for something I usually got it, with interest. When we sold the house, I quit my job and we moved in with him.

I had decided I needed to give my all to make this marriage work, and I realized that included sex. I tried to force myself to be sexual but with little luck, so I started drinking in the afternoons so I could be anything he wanted me to be when he got home. A few months later we had one of my friends down for the weekend. Late one evening she had gone into the guest bath to change clothes and I had gone to check on the children. We had had some drinks and drugs, so I was 10 feet tall and bulletproof. When I came back into the living room my husband was coming in the back door. I could not deny that he had been peeping on my friend. For the first time I confronted him. I had been consciously trying to keep him satisfied and he still was not getting enough. I knew we needed help.

A few days later, I got my first conscious miracle. While I was getting dressed the TV was on, turned to *Donahue*, and Patrick Carnes was his guest. (Patrick Carnes is an expert on sexual addiction.) I sat down in disbelief. This man was telling my story and not condemning me. A phone number was given at the end of the program and I called it. I was given the number of a local therapist who dealt with these issues. I then called my husband, all excited that I now knew what was going on; that it was a disease and we were not crazy.

God has a way of putting me where I need to be. I was away from people who expected me to behave a certain way. I was not working, and yet had access to good baby sitting.

My first Co-SA meeting was terrifying. This group was very protective and I had to go through interviews before I was allowed to attend. Two women met with me and I had to tell my story to two strangers. But as I spoke, I saw reassurance and acceptance in their eyes, and then they told me some of their stories, and told me I was welcome. They had me promise I would attend four meetings before I decided if Co-SA was for me.

The first meeting I attended was a noon meeting, mostly of business women. They came in with small talk but at 12:00 they started with a boom. One woman was yelling at God for what had happened to her, another was crying about more information she had found on her lover, and another was reading her gratitude list. Then at 12:55 they stood up and said the Lord's Prayer, got hugs and all went away.

I come from people who live the "do not talk, do not trust, do not feel" rules, and these people had broken them all. The only thing that felt comfortable was the Lord's Prayer and the hugs. But I did come back. About the third meeting I needed to talk. I didn't feel safe, but I needed to talk, and I knew they would listen and not judge. I felt great for talking and then scared, but I kept coming back.

As I worked on my therapy and my program it became apparent that my husband was only giving it lip service. My therapist and sponsor told me to keep the focus on me and try not to deny my reality. One night after I had put the kids down and had gone to bed, I had a panic attack. I realized he was in so much pain and getting so crazy that he was capable of killing me and the children, and then himself. I was petrified, I could not move, I could not even get up and check on the kids. Life was becoming more unmanageable. I had been told there was no money to buy summer clothes, yet I found a stack of new porn costing around five hundred dollars.

My therapist told me I had to put a time limit on this relationship. If things did not improve I had to leave. So I used the one year rule. He started talking about buying a house and I realized I needed to tell him I might not be staying. I told him in the therapist's office, and she quickly added that if he decided to leave earlier than the one year that I got to go to treatment. And yes, he pulled out before the year was over. I was relieved, scared, and sad—I had been with him for fifteen years.

I knew enough to do the next right thing, and treatment was it, even though it meant traveling to another state, leaving my children with someone I feared, and leaving my support group. One of the reasons I had never left before was I was afraid of that old depression. I had lived through it before, but I was not sure I could live through it this time.

My sponsor rode with me on my out of state journey to go to treatment. I felt like I was starting a new life. I was excited and overwhelmed and numb. The only thing I think I got out of the seven weeks of treatment was, "I am a precious, worthwhile, fallible child of God", and that was worth every minute of it. I was now precious.

While in treatment, I had another miracle. A former employer heard I was looking for a job and called me with an offer, which I accepted. When I left treatment I went back to my home town and my children were there waiting for me at my parents' house. But now I had a new fear: I was in my old surroundings without my support group, there being no Co-SA meetings in town.

My sponsor had told me to look at my drinking, so I took that and found an AA group. I also got involved with another therapy group. And I continued to grow. During the following year the therapy group disbanded and another one did not work out. I was getting desperate for a Co-SA meeting. I contacted my former therapist and she gave me a number for a nearby town. I called and they said the meeting was being moved to my town, and to an evening hour. I made the next meeting and now had a home group.

That summer I got a true test of my program. My daughter had been acting different, no single thing, but a lot of little stuff. I had gone to a conference, seen my former therapist and told her what was going on. She told me to get my daughter to a therapist as soon as possible—it sounded like she was being abused. I cried. I thought by leaving and creating as safe an environment as I could, nothing else bad would happen to us.

The play therapist said yes, she was being abused. The policewoman said yes, she was being abused. The District Attorney said yes, she was being abused, but she would not tell us who it was. I felt betrayed. I had done everything I felt I needed to do and my Higher Power was allowing this to happen. I felt angry: how could this happen to such a sweet three year old child? I also felt sad, knowing this would affect the rest of her life. I continued to do the next right thing, taking her to therapy, holding her after she would wake up from nightmares, and telling her affirmations.

After a while I realized I was carrying this pervert's shame. I had not been the one to abuse her, and I was not responsible for it. I was only responsible for helping my daughter deal with the abuse. We got what we needed, she felt strong for talking about the abuse and we bonded as true mother and daughter. During that time I learned what serenity is: when the world around me is totally crazy and I can still feel that my Higher Power is in control and loves me.

Well, the story keeps going. I am learning how to have an honest relationship with a man, I am sponsoring several women, and have continued with therapy. I wish I had an ending for you but, you see, my life is still going—it is not over till it's over.

5

Anne's Story

I am who I am: neither ashamed nor afraid to tell you about me and my life. For over forty years I denied even to myself that the rapes and incest had affected my life or changed my personality, but now I realize how damaged I was. I've always had happy memories of myself at three and four years old but that began to change at five and six years. I had few memories of my years between six and twelve although I had an intellectual knowledge that the sexual abuse had happened. I didn't feel anything, and it was like it happened to someone else.

At five years old I began to limp and, after a long series of doctors, I spent six weeks in Crippled Children's Hospital in Oklahoma City in traction, where I was totally cut off from my family. The first memories I have of sexual abuse were when my braces were being fitted. The man who was fitting my braces put his hand up under my dress and into my vagina. I didn't know what he was supposed to do, and tried to get away from him. My father scolded me and made me stand still. I felt so humiliated and ashamed I couldn't tell my father. This same man violated me several times.

Then my oldest brother and one of his older teenage friends took me out to "play" and sexually used me. I only wanted to play games, not be abused, but they threatened me not to tell. Fear reigned and shame took over, and I didn't feel safe to tell anyone.

The friend brought other boys over with him at times, and they would always invite me to play. Each time I wanted to be included and have friends, too. It was fun for them but it was humiliating and frightening and painful for me when, one after another, they would force their penises into my vagina. This happened at least four times, and maybe more.

I began to hide, and begged my mother to let me stay in the house. Many times she did. But when she made me go out to play, I would hide and climb trees and pretend I was invisible. I was afraid of strangers, especially boys and men, and rarely felt safe.

At ten and eighteen I was raped again. At age ten one of my girlfriends took me to see her uncle who owned a feed store, to get some candy. He took me into the back room and sexually molested me. I had no feelings about this except for hating this man and never going in his store again. At eighteen I was raped by a college law student who I thought I knew from my teen years. I soon realized he was going to hurt me. He was probably the most aggressive sex addict I've ever encountered. He knocked me down and when I tried to get away from him I skinned my knees. He bruised me during the rape.

By eighteen, I was convinced that what all men wanted was sex, and I had a hard time trusting anyone. He called and tried to manipulate me to go out with him with all kinds of promises. His phone calls came to where I had stayed for months after I went away to college, and fortunately the landlady didn't give him my new address.

I was date raped once when I was engaged at age nineteen. We were fighting over something we had planned to do. He had been trying to get me to have sex with him, and I had been more and more resistant to being forced to do something I was ashamed of, so he physically forced me to have sex during the fight.

I married a perfectly charming guy. At least he was charming and the life of the party while he was drinking, which he usually was. I thought I loved him more than life, and my life was so inhibited and dull. We had sex frequently, sometimes three times a day. I didn't know that there was anything abnormal about having sex to please him and help relieve his tension three times a day. After being gang raped as a kid, that was a breeze.

I used sex to satisfy him, but can't remember ever needing or wanting sexual satisfaction myself. I had learned not to feel it as a kid and would actually be thinking about something entirely different while, outside, my body was being used and abused. So, even though he tried to stimulate and satisfy me, I rarely responded and quickly learned that I could lie to him and he didn't know the difference.

I lived a lie with him for 28 years, never telling him he was not the first man I had sex with, or about the rapes. I was too ashamed of my earlier life and too into trying to fulfill his sexual needs and control his behavior. His drinking became more of a crisis than I had ever dreamed. He beat me up while drunk and in a rage. The doctors at the hospital told him he would die shortly if he didn't stop drinking. It scared him and he cried. I told him we could lick the drinking. Since I drank very little, I didn't have any idea how hard it would be to stop drinking, but he did get dry after about a year, and stayed dry for nearly 25 years.

Many times he used sex to deal with the tension of dry drunks and I was willing to let him. Sex wasn't as bad as the drinking and beatings, to my crazy way of thinking. And after all, wasn't that what a good wife was supposed to do? I was hiding in a "safe marriage".

My denial of the effect of sexual abuse in my childhood and my shame and fear were so great. I denied that my husband had other girlfriends, even when my own children tried to tell me. I denied his alcoholism when he wanted to start drinking socially again. I denied he could possibly be having an affair with another woman when her husband called me and told me he had been following them. "That couldn't be possible, when he was in bed with me every night. Our sex life was too perfect," I said. But he was, and our marriage deteriorated.

We separated after 26 years of marriage, still having sex at times when he would come by to see me. I finally realized he was indeed involved with another woman and also stripping us financially, so I filed for a divorce and he counter-filed. Our divorce was finally granted after 28 years of marriage.

The separation was the most painful part of my life, and yet the beginning of the most healing part. I got into therapy with a group of sexually abused women and two counselors who were most helpful. Memories became clearer and I could tell my story to people who actually believed me and said so. I remained in this group over a year, never missing a week and gaining in courage to heal further. When I quit group I had reached all the seven goals I had set for myself and had overcome much of the fear of being with people.

I started going to square dance lessons and letting my little girl outside to play. I even started to date again and found myself able to talk about why I didn't want to be in a sexual relationship and wanted to continue my healing.

Approximately three years ago, I helped form the first Co-SA (Co-dependents of Sex Addicts) group in my town. Little did I know that my healing had just begun when I began in this loving supportive Twelve Step group. I had been active in Al-Anon for three years by then, and had once again been able to intellectually identify the sexual abuse, although without any feelings.

After about one and a half years in Co-SA, I began having dreams and body feelings so frightening and real that I could hardly hold my job. The nightmares, difficulty sleeping, and body memories were surfacing after forty years of being denied and suppressed. I thought sometimes I was going crazy, but my Co-SA friends lovingly supported me, and my sponsor suggested possibly going to a therapist or entering treatment.

I was in such emotional pain I did go back to the co-therapist who had facilitated the first group of sexually abused women I was in. Gradually I verbalized what had happened, what I felt, and began sorting out the feelings for current issues from the old body memories and nightmares. I realized I hadn't had much of a childhood, because of living in fear, hiding, and not being able to trust my own family members. My healing will probably go on for the next forty years just as my suffering in shame and fear lasted so long. Recognizing my strengths to survive, being less hypervigilant, and learning healthy ways to be assertive has been such a blessing. I can laugh and play, sing and dance, and be happy, joyous and free in the moment I'm living now.

6

This Has Been
My World

I was born in a small midwestern town, population about 70,000 at its peak. I was the middle child of three children. The first two of us had the same father, the baby girl did not. My mother was handicapped emotionally, mentally and physically. She had older brothers and one younger sister. All of her brothers were alcoholic. Her younger sister was raped at the age of ten. They never found the man who did it, even though she gave a thorough description of him. She says it seemed as if it didn't matter. We both know it did.

I have reason to believe that my grandfather was a sex addict. My aunt has given me some support in piecing together my early family life, because I don't remember a lot of my growing up years. All I seem to home in on is the feeling of fear of loss: loss of life, loss of power, loss of love, loss of protection, loss of me.

My father and mother divorced early on and I don't remember Daddy ever being a part of our household. I do remember some of his visits, and particularly my visits to his house to babysit his children from his second marriage. It has been rumored that he had a daughter older than my brother somewhere in California. Nobody ever talked about her.

From what I have pieced together my father was an alcoholic, control fiend, a sex addict and a rage-aholic. He was very abusive and verbally humiliating to all of us.

My great aunt told me two things when I was about six years old. First, I was too old to be sitting on my grandfather's lap, and second, that the reason my mother yelled and mistreated me so badly was that my father had forced himself on her after they had separated and that's how she got pregnant with me. I didn't understand then, but I knew instinctively that they were bad things.

All I remember from my mother was fear of people, places and things. I also remember a tremendous amount of rage. She told me over and over as a child, "Get this, do that before I kill your stupid ass!" I never seemed to be able to do what it took to keep her from being angry with me. This is the atmosphere that I grew up in. My mother had suitors, but no more marriages. She had two more pregnancies, both of which resulted in stillborn babies.

The thing I remember most about my brother, who was the empowered one, was that he was very cruel. He was filled with being in charge, and never missed a chance to use that power to hurt, humiliate, and abuse me, my cousins and my little sister. He hurt me physically, emotionally, spiritually, and sexually. I was caught between a rock and a hard place. My mother was hearing impaired and I think she just didn't hear what she didn't want to hear. She just didn't respond to me at all.

I gave up. I just did whatever my brother decided I should do. It's no wonder that I thought all men were in power. I don't think, in all of my 39 years of life, that I've ever made decisions that weren't based on someone else's needs and/or wants instead of my own. I've spent my whole life living through someone else's opinion of who I am and who I should be. I especially have done this with the men in my life. I believe that every man I've been involved with has been a sex addict. Let me tell you my story.

By the time I was 16 or so, my spirit had been broken down to the point of nothing. I felt so much pain in my family of origin, that I knew I had to get out any way I could. I had to get out or die. I didn't know what the pain was, or that there was a reason for it. I certainly had no idea that I was not alone in my feelings. I just knew I felt it.

I met my future husband in high school. I was introduced to him and thought it was love at first sight. Hindsight tells me it was more awe and fear. He was outspoken, loud, and probably demonstrated all the things that I wish I could. My friend, and even my brother told me that he was bad news, but I didn't want to see that. I heard that he had gotten a lot of girls pregnant and that his parents had gotten him out of the situations with their money. We were very poor. I thought I had a catch.

He didn't treat me badly, and didn't abuse me—at least not in the ways I was used to being abused. He treated me with what I thought was respect. I now believe that it was part of the sex addict dance. We went to the movies, he bought me stuffed animals, and we talked. He taught me how to drive a stick-shift car, and I was grateful that he spent time with me. I was still a virgin, and told him when he brought up the sex thing. (Back then we called it the sex thing.) He said he would wait for me to say yes.

We dated for a year and I felt like I was on cloud nine. We got engaged, and had been for about eight months when I decided to give him my virginity. In December of 1967 I was deflowered. I was to graduate from high school in June 1968 and we would be married. He had graduated in 1967 and had a job working for the railroad. He was making good money, and as far as I could see, we were on the right track. I decided in January of 1968 that my home life was getting worse and I wanted out, with someone and something to call my own. I suggested that we have a baby, and he said okay.

By the time I graduated from high school I was three months pregnant. His mother asked to see me at their house, and she wanted to know what we were going to do. Back then pregnant, seventeen, and not married was not good. I then began to feel trapped. I let go of thoughts and plans to go to college, and in July 1968 we got married. His mother's hints that people would talk scared me.

It seemed the moment we signed the marriage papers our relationship changed. We moved into his mother and father's house, and prepared for the journey of married life and parenthood. Now that I think back, we never took a course in these things. We were never even told how to wing it. He became very abusive verbally, and somewhat abusive physically. Emotionally it was like I had been dating Dr. Jekyll and had married Mr. Hyde. He even accused me of having an affair with the doctor who was to deliver our child because my visits always took too long. He began drinking, staying out when he wanted to, and arguing with me all the time about everything. I was scared to death of him. I felt trapped and hopeless again.

Nobody seemed to care. His mother and father never said a word because his mother was in the same situation. His father was doing the same things to her that my husband was doing to me. No wonder my husband thought that was the way it was supposed to be. I had no role models, so I took my in-laws' silence for approval.

We moved into our own apartment about three blocks from his parents' house. His mother became highly involved in our lives. She knew things about our household that I didn't know. He naturally said that he could talk to his mother about anything. She was his confidante. Looking back, they talked about everything except the elephant that was in the living rooms of both our houses. His mother did everything to make the picture look nice and neat to the outside world. The family picture looked good on the outside. Inside, these families were the devil himself in raw form.

I was due to deliver my baby on December 22, and on the morning of December 10, my husband's mother called to say he had been injured on the job. She came to get me so we could go to the hospital. We went to see him, and later in the day I shopped for his personal items to be left at the hospital because he was injured enough to stay there. I didn't want to be alone, so I went back to stay at his parents' house. That evening I became queasy, and at 7:00 I was admitted to the same hospital my husband was in to deliver my child. She was born at 4:25 a.m. the next morning, and she was beautiful. I was scared. I now had a little life that I was responsible for rearing, and I had no clue. I was afraid.

When my husband was released from the hospital, we all went back to our little apartment. Things got more and more out of control. I went to work before he was well enough to go back to his job, and I gave him my paycheck because he said I should. I had to ask him for money to spend. Any attempt to question or stand up to him resulted in more abuse. I gave up again.

After a year or so, he got a $10,000 settlement for the injuries he had received. I saw the bank book and held it in my hands one or two times. He spent it at will (more truthfully at

Sally and Jane, etc.). I was so scared of him that I let him abuse me financially, emotionally, spiritually, and sexually.

I think his mom got him out of jail twice for drunk driving and driving without a license. He started what was to be a four year spree of drinking, drugs, and sexually acting out all over town. Everybody knew, but just didn't mention it. I guess I thought it would go away too if I just never talked about it. The pain grew worse and worse in me, and I simply didn't know what to do. I began to attend church more and more. A way out, I thought. I thought God would come down from the sky, convict him, and make him turn from his ways if I kept the faith. That never happened.

After a very ugly fight in 1972, he snatched our daughter from my arms to get at me. He hurt her. I decided that I would have to either kill him, or get out of this marriage. If I killed him and went to jail, who would take care of my daughter? The next morning after he left for work, I left.

I had no idea what I would do. At that point I was unemployed because he had talked me into quitting my job and trying to be a housewife. He wanted me to have another child, so I said okay. I had fallen for another, "I'm sorry, and I'll change," piece of rhetoric from him. He never changed and now I was really worse than I had ever been.

After I left him, I got a job, filed for divorce and got my own apartment, just my daughter and me. He pursued me more than ever. I refused to endanger my child. I really didn't know I had a right to leave for my own safety. All I could think about was my daughter.

As it turned out, he was dating all the while and was testing me, I guess. He wanted to see if he still had me in his power, because I read in the local paper he was engaged to a minister's daughter. I asked him about it and he denied even knowing the woman or her family. I'm so glad that I still was able to say no to him.

It's really strange now to look back and know that I still had sex with him after I knew he was engaged to someone else. I even asked him once if we were going to get back together. I was just as sick as he was, and for a short while, I considered letting him back into my life. I've heard that he is now a minister of his own church. It scares me, because I don't think he's gotten into any kind of recovery.

My pattern had been set. Picking men was not my forte. The next man in my life was eleven years older than me. I met him two months after I left my husband. This man pursued me for several months and I finally gave in. We became lovers. He wanted me to move in with him, but became enraged when I asked him to help me find a car for my own transportation. He broke it off. I also knew he was into smoking pot and drinking alcohol, but, in my mind, he couldn't have had a problem because he was a professional man. I knew that it was rage in our encounter about the car and it scared me enough to stay away.

After several months he called me, and I went out with him again. We had sex again, but I was distant enough that he knew it had ended for me. So did I. He had a little black book of women and he went right on dating like he hadn't missed a step of the dance. I suspect he was still seeing other women all along. It was my second look at a sex addict.

There weren't a lot of men in my life, but I did give the free Seventies a try. It just didn't feel right to meet guys and go straight to bed with them. The next one I thought I felt any love for was very nice. When he mentioned marriage, I left. Really left. Marriage terrified me. The other thing that scared me was bringing another child into this world, so I had my tubes tied.

I dated on and off but the nice ones seemed to scare me. I usually met more of the other ones—the rebels, or the strong and silent types—and those were the ones I got seriously involved with.

All the while I struggled with my religious beliefs. My prayers were, "God please just don't let me go crazy and don't let me be desperate for another relationship."

The paradox in this is that I always either was totally celibate, or I just sucked another man into my life so quickly that I didn't even know I'd done it. I seemed to just wake up one day and find myself stuck in another sick relationship. I even got a sexually transmitted disease, which I didn't even know could happen.

Over the years I knew something wasn't quite right, but I couldn't put my finger on it. I thought it was just me, so I kept trying to do better, be better for someone else. It's sick, I know, but I was set up before I was even born to relate to men this way. I had no idea what intimacy was; no idea what looking at my own stuff was about.

In 1980 I moved to another state. I guess I was running from myself, but I didn't know that then. I met a man in the church I joined, and I believe that he was the very sickest of all the sex addicts I have met. He was a liar, had been convicted of crimes, had jumped bond and broken his parole. I suspected him of sexual acting out, I suspected child abuse, I suspected he was a pedophile, but I couldn't prove any of it. I spent five years in this major crazy hurricane, and even considered marrying the man because he belonged to the church. He even lied to me about his job and what he did for a living. It was stupid stuff, yet he always had a reason to cover himself. I wanted to believe in Christian men so badly that I just refused to give myself any credit whatsoever.

When I finally talked to his second ex-wife I found out that most of my suspicions were true. The others couldn't be proven. In the beginning I thought it was refreshing for a man not to be so concerned with sex as the others in my life had been. I didn't know for a long while that he just wasn't interested in sex with adult women.

He was caught for another white collar crime, and I had to testify for the state against him. He went back to jail. This was also just after I had a complete hysterectomy and had been physically ill from that. I was so grief stricken that I threw up nearly every day for what seemed like a long time. The doctor put me on anti-depressants. I wonder why? Could I have been depressed? I was a wreck for a long time.

After a little over a year of celibacy, an old male high school friend of mine forced the introduction of my latest romance on me. He told me either I met the guy, or he would bring him over to my apartment early one Saturday or Sunday morning when he was sure I'd be embarrassed by the rollers in my hair and no make-up on my face. Well this one was another strong silent type. The sad thing is, I didn't even remember what this type was about. I started the dance one more time. By this time my daughter was old enough to move out. She had graduated from high school and we were so at odds with each other I think we both knew it was best that she leave.

I was in this last relationship for a little over five years. There must be something magic for me in the number five. For a while we dated, but looking back we didn't go a lot of places; mostly to his apartment or mine. It took a long time for me to meet any of his friends. When I did, his best friend's girlfriend told me that they thought I was the one who didn't want to meet them. It was a repeat of part of what I had experienced with the jailbird. It seemed that sex addicts have this thing to keep people in their lives separated so that one part of their lives doesn't run over into another part. I wonder why?

I gave him the benefit of the doubt. I didn't listen to me again. After three years of sex, anger, not speaking, making up and then breaking up, I was transferred to another state. Just before I left, he proposed to me. He had wanted to live together but I just couldn't do that. I said yes to marriage. I think I just didn't know how to be by myself.

I moved and he was supposed to follow me in six months. By the beginning of my second year in this new state, I realized he wasn't here yet. I even called the state for information about getting the marriage license. I forgot about one small detail: he wasn't divorced from his first wife yet. They had been apart for several years, but neither had filed for divorce.

Then I got the crazies. I thought, "I have to find out what's wrong with this picture." I was willing. I went to a support group and was able to grow some. I called my fiance, and said maybe I needed another year here alone, and he panicked. He said he'd be here as soon as he could.

By the end of my second year alone, he showed up. He moved in with me. I still had the marriage thing in the back of my mind. He knew I was changing. I finally went to a Co-SA meeting and began to work on my sexually abusive past. At home, things got worse. In hindsight once more, I believe that he was a dry alcoholic, an adult child of an alcoholic, and had sexual addiction issues.

Thirty days after he moved in I had to check into a psychiatric hospital. I had swallowed, choked on, so much humiliation, degradation, abuse, hurt and pain from almost every man in my life—from my father and brother to this last fiasco of a relationship—that even I could no longer pretend that nothing was wrong. He seemed satisfied with it, but I couldn't do it one more time. He was still willing to pretend, but he'd have to do it without me.

Three months after I got out of treatment, I asked him to move out. He stalled, I stood my ground, and he finally did move. We continued to see each other off and on, and two months ago I asked him not to contact me at all. I just couldn't work on me and a relationship with him at the same time. I was sick myself. I couldn't nurture him too. I finally admitted that there just wasn't enough of me left to go around. I needed all of me for me. He insisted that there must be someone else, and I told him that there was: ME. He said, "You know what I mean." I was able to say to him, "You tell me where in the rule book of life it says that I can't leave you for myself."

I've been so very angry these last two years: angry that nobody taught me that I DIDN'T HAVE TO PUT MY LIFE INTO SOME MAN'S HANDS; angry that nobody showed me how to think for myself and that it was okay for me to do so; angry that I was taught a good Christian woman stays with her husband no matter how badly he treats her and their children; angry because my family knew that there were problems, but nobody had the courage or insight to start looking at them and be honest; angry that I've gone through all these years of enmeshment, abuse, and pain; angry that nobody told me I had the right to express these hurts without fear of harm to me for doing so. I was angry with a capital A.

I'm in recovery today, and the Twelve Steps in Co-SA have saved my life. I'm looking at a future in which I can teach myself and my daughter that we have choices. We can have honesty, love, trust, nurturing, and intimacy, first for ourselves and then for others. I'm learning to share what I have out of love, not guilt, shame, coercion, fear, or ignorance of who is at the helm of my life. I'm learning the difference between religion and spirituality on a daily basis. I have lived my emotional and literal lives in beiges and browns so as not to rock the boat. God put pink, green, purple and yellow in the rainbow and I can choose any one or all of these colors. I HAVE A CHOICE TODAY. It's been a tough road and I've still got a long way to go, but I'm glad I started the journey. I'm getting in touch with me, and developing a personal relationship with God, one day at a time. I'm learning foresight from working through all the hindsight.

I tried to talk to my younger sister about healing the past to have a different today and a brighter future, but she seems to think that the past is just the way that people of color have lived and always will live. She says the past is "just life," as she calls one of her sons a dummy in the background of our phone conversation. She also admits that our mother merely tolerated my presence in her life. My sister would really freak if I told her that I know my father sexually abused me; I just don't have the specific picture memory of it yet. She doesn't know that surviving life and living life are two different things.

I'm here to tell that the past that I've shared with you in my story should not be, "just how it is." I've been abused in the name of everything under the sun, and like my sister, I AM OF COLOR, and my past was abusive. It was abuse.

Marie

7

Laurie's Story

My story is the result of the way I reacted to what happened to me as a child. I've been in recovery from alcoholism for over eleven years, and in the past year I've admitted also to my powerlessness over sex addiction and co-dependency with sex addicts. And what a relief it is to tell you so!

The process of recovery is ongoing, and a great adventure. As with most adventures, my own story is full of pain and fear, as well as the thrill of the discovery of new hope and a new life of miraculous wonder.

My first memories, from as early as three years of age, are of a sexual nature, with myself and various neighborhood boys as the main actors. The elements of fear, terror, attraction, and excitement are pervasive in all these memories and have been a common thread running throughout my life.

"Boys" were, and still are, real scary, real attractive people to me. Until recently, I had never considered friendship with members of the opposite sex an option. My dad was the scariest and most desirable power in my life when I was small, but he was inaccessible always, and this fact has colored my perception of males all of my life. I've always considered males to be smarter than I, tricky, superior, and POWERFUL. A gal could die for a man like that, as I've wanted, and tried to do many times over.

What I learned about myself in recovery is that, as an incest survivor, my trust was violated, and never blossomed into intimacy with the primary caregivers in my infancy. My needs for affection and protection, which foster the knowledge of my own unique preciousness, were left unfulfilled, so, as a true survivor, I found whatever means at my disposal to go about getting my own needs met. Sexualizing those needs was my primary source of power over my environment, and though it didn't EVER fill the bill, I became obsessed with making it work.

I grew up in a house that looked like a castle, complete with tower. My parents, though Dad's income was not high, are college degreed. Dad had a master's degree, and earned his Ph.D. when I was small. He was a professor in a state university. My mom, the mother of four, stayed home as homemaker. I was the youngest child, with a brother two years older and two sisters, three and six years older respectively.

I adored my father, idolized and feared his suppressed rage. When I was very small I was Daddy's girl, but I remember sometime when I was about five, my parents would no longer allow me to sit on Dad's lap after dinner. I became obsessed with regaining my cherished status. I would plot and plan ways to get his attention and acted them out. The methods I used were seductive and coy, but they were to no avail.

I remember that sometime during this year I "fell in love" with one of Dad's graduate students from England. He was attentive and caring. When I found out he was going back to England, I mustered up all my courage and asked him to take me with him. He represented safety and love, and I, for some reason, felt I just had to escape my parents, especially my dad. This was my way out. I was devastated when he gently refused. The adults laughed and thought it was so cute, but I was truly bereft. I was trapped at home and there was no way I'd ever be rescued, freed. I know today that it was strange for a five year old to feel that her home was a place to get away from.

Every male/female relationship I've had which seemed significant mirrors that same scenario until now, until recovery, when things are beginning to change. It's different today, thank God, Co-SA, and the Twelve Steps. But before, if a boy, or a man, was interested in me and didn't respond to my seductiveness, he didn't have a chance with me. What I didn't realize until recently is that if a man or boy *did* respond to my seduction, I would end up emotionally abandoned and used as a sex object. I "knew" somehow, that that's all a man would be interested in me for anyway, and using the power of the sexual high to "keep my man" kept me feeling in control and much less vulnerable. The high, though, always bottomed out, and I'd be left feeling not only vulnerable, but also "used." It has only been in recovery that I've understood how I set that up and perpetrated it in so many of the relationships I had with men.

I started to become aware of the fact that perhaps I was setting these deals up myself, even to the point of picking, or allowing myself to be picked by the "leading man of the year," so to speak. This awareness began to come to me when I was 35 years old, and three years sober in Alcoholics Anonymous.

The Twelve Steps have changed the lives of many people, myself and my women friends included. I had worked at practicing the Steps through studying them and listening to others' experiences, and at 35 my life was centered around the practice of the Steps in daily living. My thirteen year old son, who had been living with my ex-husband since he was four, came to live with me. I awakened to the fact that I had some true emotional disorders which hadn't disappeared just because I'd stopped drinking. I'd cried rivers over the remorse and guilt I felt about my sexual acting out while I was drinking, but the *shame*, the shame just kept surfacing over and over again no matter how many inventories I wrote or how much I prayed.

I decided to be "good," one more time. Each time I got "good" I'd let go of more and more of my own unique forms of self-expression in the bargain. If the way to escape this shame was to stop being sexual with anyone at all, then I'd do it, drastic as it seemed. Maybe then God could accept me into His Kingdom. I threw myself into motherhood. I joined a five year Bible study and worked it lovingly and diligently. At least I was acceptable. I threw myself into my work, teaching first graders and, one day at a time, grieved the loss of my "sexuality." I was very careful to avoid sending out "vibes" to men. I found that I had no way of relating to men at all without coy, seductive "cuteness." My fear and anger toward males began to surface and I avoided getting to know new men. I fielded the advances of others. I began to see that all but one of my men friends were sexually abusive and emotionally unavailable. I quit wearing make-up and gained ten pounds. I wore clothes which left my gender in question. I began to wonder if I were secretly gay, even though I'd never acted out that way.

My relationship with Todd, my son, became very important to me. I realized my parenting skills were inadequate, and much of the time we behaved as if we couldn't stand each other. I went to see the lay psychologist at the Catholic school where I was a teacher about my problems relating to Todd, and as I see it now, it was another example of how God guides me to the truth if I'll be just vaguely open to it.

I spoke to the woman psychologist about my reasons for coming to see her. I responded to her questions, and after I'd talked for about twenty minutes she said to me, "Laurie, I'm leading a six week group therapy for women who've been sexually abused as children. I think you'd benefit from attending. Would you like to?"

I was mystified. I'd gone to this woman about my fourteen year old, and she invited me to attend a group for abuse victims. "I haven't been abused, except maybe emotionally neglected. Why me?" I asked.

She explained patiently that perhaps the abuse was more extensive than I realized, and that she knew I could benefit from the group. So I said yes. I'd prayed for guidance before coming to her and, who knows, maybe I'd learn something.

I stayed in denial through the first four sessions of that group. I listened to the others and felt sorry for their sad tales, but knew I didn't belong there. Then, during the fifth session, the truth came out in a rather remarkable way.

It was my turn to talk, so I said, "Well, I guess it's true that my dad sexually abused me..."

"Say that again," said the group leader, Sherry.

"My dad sexually abused me," I repeated.

"Again!"

Anger, rebellion welled up inside me and spilled out in the form of a frightened eight year old Laurie. "I don't want to! My daddy wouldn't do that!" I began hyperventilating and crying. Sherry moved very close and took me in her arms.

Holding me while I cried and struggled for breath, she gently spoke. "That's the front your family has put up all these years. But it's a lie. He did do 'that'. He did."

Since that time six years ago, I have been dealing with the truth. I struggled mightily with denial for much of that time. I protected myself from men by staying away most of the time, but

I had one brief romance which caused me to seek out a therapist and another affair which lasted a year. At the bitter end of that affair I spent six weeks in a treatment center for post traumatic stress disorder, i.e. sexual trauma. Some memories of the incest emerged during therapy. Mostly they are sensory memories, re-experiencing the events physically rather than cognitively.

I strive today to live a shame-free life, one day at a time. I am learning to date! There are men in my life who just enjoy my company, who keep coming around. We decide together that we're not ready for a sexual relationship. We spend time together, allow ourselves to nurture and be nurtured, and don't rush things.

Sometimes I feel so *vulnerable*. Always before with men I knew when to move in sexually and "gain control" of the situation, at least for the moment. Now I have to struggle with feeling "bored', not knowing what to say, speaking my genuine feelings and genuine thoughts. Sometimes it feels like I'm jumping off the high dive, not knowing whether there's water in the pool or not. But so far I've survived becoming real. My inner child and I are trusting each other, and I'm a trustworthy parent and adult for her most of the time.

If you've read this far, you know me well. I'd love to know you, too. Hope to see you at a meeting! We all have a lot of painful memories. Let's share them, and then get on with LIVING!

Laurie

Part II—Our Similarities

8

Dysfunctional Family of Origin

Your family of origin is the family you grew up in. It would probably be safe to say that healthy families do not produce women who are attracted to sexual addicts. As adults, we are attracted to situations that feel "normal" to us. If you are from a healthy family, and you come across a sex addict, you recognize that there is something wrong with the picture and you leave.

Not so for women who love sex addicts. Most of these women grew up in dysfunctional families where the "don't talk, don't trust, don't feel" rule was adhered to. A woman who loves a sex addict can see, and even participate in sexual behavior that at some level feels "wrong" to her, and stay in the situation because it feels normal: it is just like home.

At home, when there was abuse, nobody talked about it. If they did, they were not believed, and they learned to not trust their own perceptions, or that the grown-ups in charge could not be trusted to take care of them. As a result, the overwhelming feelings of hurt, sadness, and shame were denied and repressed. Feeling anything became unsafe. The woman who finds herself living with a sex addict as an adult just continues to follow those same old rules.

What was home like for these women when they were children? Many have family histories where sexual addiction, or other addictions, were present: alcoholism, drug addiction, eating disorders, workaholism, religious addiction. In an active addictive family system, members are encouraged to ignore and deny inappropriate behaviors. Children are not allowed to express their feelings about what is going on, and learn to deny not only their reality, but how they feel about it. It becomes a perfect set-up for living in a sexually addictive system: my spouse is doing and saying some things to me or others that don't seem right, but I can't talk about it or even really admit it to myself.

One woman, who was new to a recovery group for sexual co-dependents, asked the group if any of them had ignored any "red flags" that indicated sexual addiction before they got married or became involved with the sex addict. Another member responded, "I didn't just pass them up, I made a skirt out of them." We do the best what we've done the longest, and this woman was used to ignoring warning signs. She learned it in her family of origin.

An overwhelming number of sexual co-dependents come from families where they were abused. Some were abused physically or emotionally, but many more abused sexually. Childhood sexual trauma is probably the single most prevalent historical similarity for women who are involved with sex addicts as adults. Many of these women have suppressed their memories of abuse, however, or the abuse may have happened when she was a baby, and not be subject to conscious recall. It is not uncommon for a woman, who enters therapy to deal with

72

her husband's sexual addiction, to discover childhood abuse which predisposed her to pick a sex addict in the first place. It is a spiritual axiom that whatever we run from, we run to. If we have suppressed memories of childhood sexual abuse, or if we refuse to deal with the memories we do have, we will be attracted to situations where the issue will come up again. Or, for some women, again and again. What better place to do that than in a marriage with a sex addict?

There are women who honestly cannot identify sexual abuse issues. In their families, nobody ever talked about sex. (Some professionals consider this a form of sexual abuse.) They made it to their wedding nights knowing absolutely nothing about sex except that it was their wifely duty to submit to their husband. Perhaps they didn't even have that guideline to follow. They were entirely innocent and naive. When the sex addict they married presented his sexual behavior as normal, they believed him. A woman we interviewed identified herself as a naive nineteen year old when she married her first sex addict. He told her that she had just lived a sheltered life, and that everyone had extramarital sex and went to porno movies, and that all men had sex with other men at times. She just needed to grow up and get with it.

Sexual addiction is progressive, and the initial acting out behavior may not have been extreme in nature. As the addiction progresses, and these women become more and more uncomfortable with the addict's behaviors, they may sincerely believe that there is something wrong with themselves. The sex addict will certainly allow them to believe this, and the women will probably still not have a support system where it is okay to discuss sex. They take a little different path, but end up at the same place as the women who were sexually abused: hurt, confused, depressed and isolated.

9

Low Self Esteem

The family of origin for many women who love sex addicts was rigid. Some had little display of affection. Still others had family secrets about a parent or sibling's behavior. This rigidity, combined with restrictions that did not allow the young woman to do her own thinking, often set the stage for problems with self esteem.

Women who love sex addicts frequently say they "don't feel good about themselves." They experience what we call low self esteem. This is a feeling that, "I am not as good as, or not equal to, other people I know." In their relationships, these women feel "less than" or "one down" from the sex addict they are dating or are married to.

The truth is, we are attracted to partners with self esteem similar to our own. Sex addicts are usually trying to increase their sense of value through their addiction. At the core of the sex addict is a belief that, "nobody would love me just as I am if they really knew me."

This feeling of being unworthy of love for who she is instead of what she does, is also part of the low self esteem for the woman who loves a sex addict. Most significant, though, is her belief that her value lies in being "enough" for the sex addict.

We live in a culture where we are encouraged to believe that outer appearances and behaviors determine our value. Women who love sex addicts frequently believe that if they were only more (or in some cases less) attractive, sexy, intelligent, shapely, submissive, or better in bed, they could alter the addict's behavior. Their self esteem, which may already have been damaged as a result of childhood abuse, falls even lower as they become more and more involved in trying to fill the insatiable needs of the addict by changing themselves.

Society imparts a strong message to a woman that, if there is something wrong with her relationship, there is something wrong with her. The sex addict is usually only too happy to confirm this belief. In addition, many therapists, not understanding the dynamics of sexual addiction and sexual co-dependency, unknowingly reinforce this societal message. One woman sought help from two counselors, who told her to go home and satisfy her husband's sexual desires, and all her marital problems would disappear. Of course she failed, thereby proving to herself, one more time, that she was not good enough.

The co-addict is not only subjected to sexual put-downs, she is also frequently a victim of emotional and verbal abuse from the addict as well. Over time, she will begin to believe what the sex addict tells her about herself is true. Like the addict, she will harbor a secret belief that nobody will love her for who she is, but only for what she does. Unable to gain a sense of worth by being sexual enough for the addict, a woman can often be found taking care of not only the addict, but her kids, her family of origin, even her neighbors, in a search for worth that she can only experience in a spiritual recovery program and in the loving eyes of other accepting, recovering women.

Low self esteem is the natural outcome of loving a sex addict, and probably, at least in part, the cause of being attracted to one in the first place. Like many of the characteristics yet to be discussed, it is a core recovery issue for women who love sex addicts.

10

Black and White Thinking

Living in an addictive system creates and perpetuates many extremely unhealthy patterns of thinking and feeling. One of these patterns is all or nothing, black and white thinking. Most addicts and co-addicts live, think, and feel in extremes. They understand feeling way up or way down, but are uncomfortable just feeling OK. They understand good and bad, but have difficulty with the concept that every human being has both good and bad qualities. They believe they have to have it all, or they can have nothing. In a relationship with a sex addict this is manifested in a number of ways.

One example of black and white thinking is when the woman who loves a sex addict sees the addict as either all good or all bad. She can focus on his sexual acting out as evidence that he is no good, thereby creating some sense of esteem for herself (at least she's not doing those terrible things). This works as long as the sex addict is acting out. When he does something kind or loving, however, she will feel confused and switch to thinking she was all wrong about him and that he is indeed all good. Or, he will deny that he is acting out, and out of a need to believe in his goodness she will discount evidence to the contrary, no matter how obvious it is. Always focused on whether he is good or bad, she will be unable to focus on herself and make decisions about her own behavior, or value herself independently of who the addict is today.

Another example of a black and white, all or nothing belief system is reflected in the woman who believes she is either all good or all bad. At any given moment, her behavior will reflect whether she believes she is good (often exhibited as a holier than thou attitude, or grandiosity), or bad ("I'm worthless and deserve to be treated as such"). On the other hand, this woman can feel all "bad" on the inside and be compelled to project an image of being all "good" on the outside. She will frequently insist that her family members do the same thing, and be intolerant of behaviors in herself or others which disturb the surface image of a "good" family. She understands feeling perfect and feeling worthless, but nothing in between. Anything less than perfect is worthless, in herself or in others. Because of this, she can either love herself or hate herself, and love others or hate others, but leaves herself no room for other emotions. It's an exhausting existence, a real emotional roller coaster, and a frightening ride through life.

In the area of behaviors, black and white thinking again produces extremes. The woman who loves a sex addict will decide one day to leave, and the next day to stay with her addict. She will make promises to herself and threats to the addict about things she will and will not put up with, then not be able to follow through. She will alternate between elation when things are going her way, and depression when they are not.

For example, she will set boundaries with the addict about a particular sex act, and unrealistically expect that she will be able to maintain her new boundaries. Having made the decision, she will feel good about herself until she meets with the addict's insistence that she participate as she always has. Not having any way to say no, she will give in and one more time shame herself and feel worthless. Black and white thinking is a no win situation for the woman who loves sex addicts, leading to constant inconsistencies in feelings and behavior, and perpetuating the trap of the addictive system.

When it comes to expressing feelings, this all or nothing phenomenon can result in one partner expressing all the feelings in the relationship, and the other remaining shut down. Or, there may be certain feelings that are permissible for one member to express, but not the other. Generally in our society women are allowed the expression of sadness, but not anger. Men are more frequently allowed to express anger but not sadness.

In the relationship with the sex addicted partner, this can be taken to extremes. For example, Becky rarely had to express her own anger—she would just tell her sex addict husband what had upset her and he would rage. Afraid of her own anger—much of which would be directed at him, and possibly destroy the relationship if it was expressed—Becky chose work addiction as a way to run from her feelings, and allowed her husband to express all the anger in their household.

In her relationship, Ellen could cry, and in fact cried about a lot of things, a lot of the time. This allowed her husband to focus on what he termed her "emotional weaknesses" and appear to be the one in control. He convinced her that she would be unable to cope in the world alone, and she stayed stuck in a relationship where his sexual acting out put her at risk.

Even when we look at the woman who loves sex addicts in a situation that does not directly involve an addict, this all or nothing approach is evident. Some women spend the majority of their time appearing extremely, even unnaturally calm, competent and in control. Then, something will trigger an emotional outburst that seems out of proportion to the situation at hand. Julie was a single mother, very capable at her job, who had been in a recovery program for several years. She was dealing with her daughter's pending summer visit to her father, and found herself in a family therapy session terrified and unable to stop crying. This was a side of herself Julie rarely allowed herself, much less others, to see. She was as surprised as the therapist at the intensity of her feelings, and was able to recognize that she had been sending her daughter to visit her sexually addicted ex-husband twice a year for years, without ever acknowledging to herself the terror that it created within her.

Julie had dealt to some extent with her own childhood abuse, but had never really addressed the sexual abuse she experienced in that marriage. To have acknowledged the feelings around that would not have fit with her image of a woman in control of her feelings. It was okay to express the feelings of her own inner child (it's okay for kids to cry), but it was unacceptable that an adult would cry uncontrollably.

Like Julie, many women have been cut off from their feelings for so long that they are terrified of expressing them at all. They are afraid of being overwhelmed. The desire to control feelings is very strong, and long suppressed feelings have a tendency to surface when we least expect or desire them. To the woman who has never allowed herself to express her feelings, even the tiniest hint of emotionality is automatically repressed. Her feelings don't just disappear though, and will show up somewhere. This is the woman who is likely to have ulcers or other stress related disorders.

Contrast this with the co-sex addict whose job it is to express everyone's feelings. She has no idea which feelings are hers and which ones belong to someone else. She just acts them all out. She is often labeled neurotic, and appears emotionally out of control much of the time. Her responses in most situations are out of proportion to the events that are occurring. People tell her that she overreacts, and may spend considerable effort trying to calm her down. She may be accused of just wanting attention, and may shame herself for her behavior, all the while not knowing herself why she reacts so strongly to things. She doesn't understand that the people around her are relying on her to express all their strong emotions for them. This can be particularly true of the addict she is married to or involved with. He is avoiding his emotions by acting out his addiction. She senses his feelings, and acts them out for him. She is likely to be attracted to the "strong, silent" types, and with good reason. It keeps them feeling strong and silent, and superior, while she just looks emotionally messy.

The end result of black and white thinking, as with other behaviors we are discussing, is a life of unmanageability, either outwardly apparent, or in the woman's inner life. With her thinking, feeling, or behavior out of control, the woman who loves sex addicts will find other things to control.

11

The Need To Control

The need to be in control is another core issue for women who love sex addicts. The evidence of the need to control can vary from person to person, but the underlying compulsion is the same: the people, places, and things in her outer world must be arranged in a specific way for this woman to feel a sense of identity, value, and safety.

When you grow up in a household where the adults are out of control because of addictions or other emotional problems, or where you face the threat of abuse, you develop a strong desire to control the things that are available to you to control. The same is true if you find yourself living as an adult in a relationship where another adult is out of control. It's just human nature: when we give up control or have control taken from us in one area of our lives, we will pick up the slack in another area.

Women whose first sexual experience, often as a young child, was with an abuser, lose their natural right to develop a healthy sexuality. They lose sovereignty over their physical bodies. In response, they control what they can.

Many develop eating disorders. A compulsive overeater might use food to control her body size, thereby keeping others at a safe distance, or eat as a way to soothe herself when she is hurt or upset. An anorexic or bulimic may not have been able to control what was done to her, but she can control what goes into her body.

One adult bulimic, a college student, realized that, after working with a man who made sexually suggestive comments to her on a regular basis, she would go home and binge. She was in a recovery program for the eating disorder, and was really hard on herself for what she considered a relapse before she made the connection between feeling violated by this man's behavior and needing to binge. Once she began to acknowledge her feelings, and discover their origin in her childhood, she could nurture her frightened inner child in healthier ways, and was less likely to binge.

People pleasing can be another form of control. Many women who love sex addicts learned at a young age to please people, no matter the cost to themselves, in order to avoid further abuse. Some learned to be "perfect" in appearance or behavior, possibly believing if they were only good enough the abuse would stop. As an adult, this kind of people pleasing can be expressed in a variety of behaviors. One woman was always up, dressed, and had her make-up on every morning for years, so her husband would never see her looking less than lovely. She was afraid he would find someone more attractive. Unfortunately, her efforts did not keep him from having an affair which nearly destroyed their marriage.

Many women will give in to sex with the addict in order to attain such necessities as being allowed to eat or sleep. Some will wear clothes they are uncomfortable with, or participate in sexual activities that feel shaming, in order to please the addict and not be abandoned, or to keep him from acting out.

The people pleasing , however, does not just involve the sex addict. It can extend to other areas of a woman's life as well. She feels compelled to put herself second to just about everyone. Because the inner, feeling environment of the woman who loves sex addicts is often out of control (whether she admits it to herself or not), and because the sex addict continues to act out his addiction no matter what she does to prevent it, she can go to great lengths to control her home or work environments. Some women have "perfect" houses, "perfect" children, "perfect" hairstyles, and make-up, and wardrobes. Others are compulsive on the job, having a strong need to be the best at whatever they do. At the other extreme is Becky, who described herself as a reverse perfectionist. She knew her house could never be perfect, so she made sure it was just the opposite, and rarely cleaned it. As she grew in her recovery, she recognized another important factor: if her house was messy and there were a lot of things cluttering the floor, an abuser would be less likely to come into her room at night. Becky, as an incest survivor, found a creative way to control her environment and protect herself. Instead of being upset with herself because she couldn't seem to keep her house clean, Becky began to see that her behavior really made perfect sense and, in fact, showed a remarkable ability to survive a really tough situation.

Becky's story illustrates an important point. Many of the "symptoms" and "characteristics" evidenced by women who love sex addicts are merely coping strategies they developed as children, which have helped them to survive threatening situations. When seen as such, these actions feel much less shaming. What it is important for each woman to recognize is that these behaviors are no longer serving her, but are in fact creating more pain and chaos in her life. Many women do reach the point where they recognize that what they have been doing is no longer working, yet they still feel helpless to stop. This can be an emotional "bottom" that can cause a woman to reach out for help, and begin to recover from the effects of living with a sex addict.

12

Boundaries

Boundaries in relationships are about knowing "where I end and where you begin". A boundary defines how far you will allow someone to come into your space. Women who love sex addicts rarely have healthy, intact boundaries. Many don't realize they have a right to boundaries at all, and have difficulty recognizing when they have violated someone else's boundaries. Their boundary systems may have been damaged in childhood, through abuse and the denial of reality that comes from dysfunctional families, or they may simply be damaged from having lived with a sex addict. Whatever the case, their physical, emotional, intellectual, spiritual, and financial boundaries are sure to need repair.

The following lists illustrate different types of boundary violations reported by the women who love sex addicts who were interviewed for this book:

Physical Boundary Violations

- Somebody invading your "space"
- Being touched without being asked first
- Being told what you can or cannot wear
- Not being allowed to cut your hair
- Being restricted in how much make-up you wear
- Being denied food or being forced to eat

- Not being allowed to come and go at will
- Being pushed, shoved, slapped, bitten, kicked, hit, punched, or choked
- Being tickled without permission
- Being threatened with a weapon
- Being forced to stay awake
- Being raped (Rape is not about sex, it's about anger and control.)

Emotional Boundary Violations

- Being told, "you shouldn't feel that way"
- Having your feelings ignored
- Being exposed to jealous anger
- Being threatened with abandonment or with being forced to leave
- Being called names
- Having affection withheld
- Being exposed to uncontrolled rage
- Being told you are responsible for someone else's feelings (You made me angry, sad, embarrassed, etc.)
- Being exposed to constant whining or pouting
- Not being allowed to cry
- Being forced to stuff your feelings out of fear of violence

Spiritual Boundary Violations

- Being forced into the role of mother or Higher Power to the addict
- Having your relationship with your Higher Power decided for you

- Having the addict act as your parent or Higher Power
- Being manipulated and controlled by others through religion

Intellectual Boundary Violations

- Being told you are crazy
- Being told you are stupid
- Having your ability to reason things out for yourself discounted
- Not being allowed to go back to school or work
- Being told you will fail
- Being blamed for your children's failures
- Having your parenting abilities discounted
- Not being allowed to make everyday choices
- Having your speech or grammar constantly corrected
- Having words put in your mouth

Financial Boundary Violations

- Not being allowed to earn or spend your own money
- Paying for necessities when the addict spent all his money on pornography
- Allowing the addict to take money from you to support his habit
- Being forced to account for every cent you spend
- Allowing the addict's spending to interfere with yours or your children's welfare or health

Sexual Boundaries

Sexual boundaries can be some of the hardest to identify and maintain for women who love sex addicts. Being around a sex addict just seems to make any sexual boundaries these women might have dissolve. They find themselves being sexual with or without conscious knowledge that they don't want to be. They become paralyzed by fear, and totally unable to protect themselves. Giving away their power is their automatic response to men in general, and to sex addicts in particular.

Although our society encourages women to give their power away to men routinely, for women who love sex addicts this giving up of personal power is most often a direct result of having been sexually or emotionally abused as a child. These women find themselves time and time again in a powerless position, and each time they may strongly desire to set a boundary, yet be unable to. In that moment they may feel like a child: frightened, alone, defenseless, unable to make appropriate decisions and act on them. Afterwards they blame themselves, not the sex addict, for the boundary violation, just as they did when, as children, they took responsibility for the abuser's behavior. Each sexual boundary violation becomes a re-enactment of the childhood abuse. In recovery, each situation that involves a sexual boundary violation, or indeed any boundary violation, becomes an opportunity for healing.

Sexual Boundary Violations

- Not respecting your right to say no to sex
- Touching you in a sexual way without permission
- Making demeaning comments about women

- Treating you (or any woman) as a sex object
- Criticizing you sexually
- Withholding affection and sex
- Exposing you to pornography
- Insisting you wear sexual clothing that you are uncomfortable with
- Expressing interest in other women when with you
- Sexualizing affectionate touch from you
- Unsolicited comments from any man about your body
- Unwanted staring from a man
- Demanding sex, or certain types of sexual acts
- Minimizing or ignoring your feelings about sex
- Having affairs outside of an established relationship
- Exposing you to sexually transmitted diseases
- Sadistic sex
- Making sexual jokes
- Buying you sexual clothing as gifts without your consent (This is really a gift for him.)
- Continually asking for a specific sexual behavior that he knows you are uncomfortable with
- Being physically forced to perform, or threatened with harm if you do not perform

These lists are by no means complete. Boundary violations are the rule, not the exception, in a relationship with a sex addict. Don't be alarmed at how damaged your boundaries have been. You've probably been in some denial about your situation for a long time. For now, just know that, with time and support, you can repair your damaged boundaries.

13

Denial

In sexual co-dependency, as in any addictive/compulsive disorder, denial is a primary symptom. Denial is a necessary survival mechanism used in a variety of diseases or traumas. As part of an overall grieving process, denial is one of the first defenses individuals experiencing trauma use in an attempt to deal with a painful reality. Having a husband who is a sex addict is most certainly a painful reality for most women.

In brief, the grieving process is as follows:

Shock	Feeling numb, almost beyond feelings
Denial	Not believing it: "It is too painful, so I'll just say it doesn't exist."
Anger	"I hate God or them for letting this happen."
Bargaining	"If I had only been a better wife, better lover, or skinnier, this wouldn't have happened."
Sorrow/ Depression	Feeling sad for the situation.
Acceptance	Accepting the reality, and making healthy choices.

Many aspects of this grieving process will be addressed in the "Solutions" section of the book. For now, we will focus on denial.

For women who love sex addicts, denial can be the hardest part of this grieving process. Women who love sex addicts deny that there is anything wrong with their spouse, their relationships, their lives. Many look well put together on the outside, but are struggling hard to keep up the facade of having everything under control.

They are extremely good at denying the visible proof of sexual addiction: pornography, time and money unaccounted for, diseases they contract from their husbands. One woman, when told by her gynecologist that she had a sexually transmitted disease, determined that she had contracted it from a toilet seat, and never even discussed it with her husband. She just knew there was no way he could have been exposed to it, even when her doctor told her that was most likely. Only several years later, when her husband was confronted by a family member about abuse of his niece, did the truth come out. This was the woman's denial, not the sex addict's.

Women who love sex addicts don't just deny what's going on around them, they deny what's going on inside them. Most are extremely out of touch with their feelings, and use a variety of compulsive behaviors to keep painful emotions out of their immediate consciousness. They may eat or sleep too little or too much, overspend, abuse chemicals, constantly keep busy and compulsively clean things. Many of these women's lives might not look unmanageable on the outside, especially if they have been responsible for keeping a family going. If they ever stopped long enough to notice, their inner lives would be full of unacknowledged emotional pain.

Acknowledging reality can be very painful, and many women want to avoid this pain. Denial is the method they use to avoid feeling it. Have you ever done any of the following?

- Said, "He is Mr. Charming and Wonderful, so how could he have such a problem?"
- Only looked at the good he did, and never asked where he had been or what he was doing.
- Internalized the problem, saying, "If he has a sex problem that means there is something wrong with me."
- Been too embarrassed to even think about him having a problem when you had such a "happy family".
- Believed all men want sex a lot, and that's just the way they are.
- Said, "He was my first sex partner and he is more experienced, so this sexual behavior must be normal."
- Having grown up in a sheltered lifestyle, believed that this must be how real people have sex.
- Told yourself, "I married him so I am stuck with this. I made my bed and now I have to lay in it."
- Said, "Well, at least he doesn't drink or smoke or beat me." (This minimizes his sexual acting out.)
- Said, "Well, he just has a stronger sex drive than I do."
- Rationalized that, "He is just being considerate not to bother me, that is why he masturbates late at night."
- Said, "I know he'd never do anything to the kids."
- Told yourself, "He deserves some time for himself. He works so hard you know."

These statements, and many like them, are prime examples of denial. Denial is powerful. Unfortunately, avoiding pain through denial prevents us from seeing the obvious. It keeps us from identifying the clues the addict may be leaving, because he wants to be caught, wants to get help.

This denial is deadly, not only to the marriage, but to the entire family. If denial is never outgrown, it can have serious consequences:

- It can leave the sex addict a woman loves in the most isolated pain he can endure: the shaming of his sexual being on a regular basis.
- It can allow other members of the family to act out sexually addictive lifestyles without ever being noticed by the parents.
- Finally, denial can lead to the addict sexually victimizing any of the children—male or female—with the mother believing the father, while the children endure the painful reality of being sexually abused at Dad's whims.

It is necessary to struggle through the grief, and acknowledge these painful realities, as we will discuss in the "Solutions" section. For as long as denial exists, reality does not.

14

Dependency and Independency

Many women who love sex addicts have never fully matured on an emotional level. Those who were abused often stopped their development at the age of their first abuse: they may look like adults on the outside, but feel like children on the inside. Women who have other addictive disorders, such as alcohol or drug abuse, may have stopped developing emotionally with the onset of that addiction. As a result, they may be stuck in either dependent or independent stages of development.

Dependency is a common theme in the stories of women who love sex addicts, and yet there seem to be two extremes in their discussions of dependency.

One type of dependency often seen in the lives of these women is called co-dependency or, in some cases, total dependency. The co-dependent woman chooses to place herself in a dependent relationship with her sex addict lover or husband, in various areas of their lives.

Co-dependency will show in a woman's need to have her sex addict partner make her feel good about herself. She often has low self-esteem, and can't really believe she is worth being loved and enjoyed as the person God created her to be. When a sex addict charms her in the beginning stages of a relationship, and tells her how special, beautiful, and good in bed she is, she feels loved and important for perhaps the first time in her life. She will stay in the roughest of relationships, put up with, and even perform, sexual acts she doesn't feel comfortable with, rather than face the loneliness and sense of worthlessness that she experiences when she has nobody to love her.

This dependency will also be evident in her social life. Many women who love sex addicts who are in this co-dependent, or total dependency, type of relationship will have limited or even non-existent relationships outside of the one they share with the sex addict. This social dependency means that she finds herself relating only to the friends of the sex addict or his family. It never occurs to her in the dependency stage that she really wants and needs her own friends. Some women who love sex addicts try to develop friendships, but give them up the moment the sex addict disapproves.

Social dependency can lead to the most frightening isolation. Some women might lose important friends—possibly after the friends have seen some of the sex addict's behavior, been sexually "hit on" by him, or even had an affair with the sex addict.

Life can become a living nightmare for the dependent woman who loves a sex addict. She feels an even greater pressure, though, if her total dependency includes being financially dependent. This is a very powerless position for the woman who loves a sex addict. They think, "What can I do anyway? I don't work, and I don't make enough to support myself, let alone my children." They may have exhausted all other financial resources, and be too ashamed to run back home to their parents, or to call an old friend, for fear of someone saying, "I told you so."

One more type of total dependency is "dependency for thought." In this type of dependency the woman who loves a sex addict gives up her freedom to think, or to believe in what is right or wrong, good or bad, or just not OK with her. This dependency is the hardest to break away from. It manifests itself in the woman's fear of what the sex addict will do if she starts taking care of her own needs, and going with her internal feelings about what is good for herself. She is afraid he will leave her, go masturbate, go to a peep show, or have an affair. The list of what he might do goes on and on. If the woman who loves a sex addict is to gain any sanity, she must first overcome her dependency for thought.

No discussion of dependency is complete without a discussion of sexual dependency. Sexual dependency means allowing the woman's sexuality and sexual needs to be defined by the sex addict. Women who love sex addicts often allow their sexuality to be suppressed to the point of non-existence in an attempt to meet the standards of performance the sex addict defines as "good enough" for him.

This surrender of her own sexuality can leave a woman without a clue as to how often she really wants to have sex. Sexual dependency can also blind a woman to whether or not she wants to be the pursued or the pursuer in the relationship. When she hears from the addict, "You're not a real woman," or, "You've lived such a sheltered life," she may begin to question, and then avoid responsibility for her own sexual boundaries. One woman's stated goal when she started recovery was to discover and define her own sexuality. She was 36 years old.

The eventual disintegration of sexual boundaries, combined with a dependent relationship, causes women who love sex addicts to perform sexual acts that they are not sure are okay, and which they later feel shame about. Lacking a sense of her own sexuality, the woman who loves a sex addict may be more open to being talked into multiple partners, or even homosexual experiences which she feels shame about later.

The sex addict can then use her guilt and shame to force her to continue a certain sexual behavior, or to lure her into even more bizarre sexual acts. Giving up her sexuality often causes the woman to feel anger toward, distance from, and a diminishing desire to even have a sexual relationship with the sex addict. When a woman feels exploited it is usually an undeniable cue that she has surrendered her individual sexuality in her relationship with a sex addict.

While these women who love sex addicts are dealing with problems of self-esteem, social, thought, and sexual dependency on the addict, there is another side of the room where women are quietly vomiting at the thought of being dependent on anyone, especially the sex addict they have a current relationship with.

These women who love sex addicts appear to have great self esteem. They look good, and may even have professional careers, but these women have only reached the second developmental stage, which is independence. They may look great on the outside but, like most adolescents, are emotionally insecure. They need to be loved, but are not able to admit to their needs. Like many adolescents, they can't ask for a hug, even though they may need one desperately.

The independent woman is often experiencing several internal struggles. When it comes to self-esteem she looks good; often she looks perfect. She is the one with color coordinated everything, including accessories. She desperately attempts to control how others perceive her. She often exhibits very controlled emotions. She may have the reputation of being "cool, calm, and collected." But this surface appearance is only one side of this woman's coin. The side she keeps hidden is the insecure side. She can't trust others with her real feelings of hurt, self-disappointment, inadequacy, and nervousness. She has to look good, and this need creates a serious dilemma for her.

The independent woman who loves sex addicts creates walls of mistrust to cover her low self-esteem. She doubts most people, their thoughts, and their motives toward her. She is often ashamed, but will cover her shame with logic or aggression in her relationships.

Because she can't trust others the woman who loves sex addicts finds she must be independent; she is the only person she can trust. Yet, she knows that sometimes she can't even trust herself, because she continues to pick men who can see her genuinely low self-esteem, and exploit her. It's a scary scenario for her when she can't trust herself, yet can't trust others either. This lack of trust is a symptom of independency and a need for control.

The social side of the independent woman who loves sex addicts also covers an internal struggle. This woman has a desperate need to look good. To enhance her low self-esteem, she finds a man who helps her look good. The sex addict may have some really positive qualities. Perhaps he is incredibly good looking, or well built. He may have money, or look like he has money. He may be the "great catch" at the office, or some other social group.

Once the woman establishes a relationship with her new sex addict, her need to control how the sex addict sees her becomes very evident. She often will change entire groups of friends when she meets her new sex addict. She often tries to control the perceptions of the sex addict's friends as well.

The "everything is wonderful" drama commonly characterizes the behavior of this woman. After all, how could somebody as smart as she is pick anyone less than wonderful? As the sex addict she chooses begins to look less desirable, she may be able to break off the relationship more quickly than her totally dependent friends. This would be a positive sign, except for the fact that a few days or weeks later she will find another sex addict who is wonderful for her self-esteem and her social needs. The drama continues, but with a different group to impress, control, and hope for acceptance from.

The thought dependency dilemma for the independent woman is similar to her problem with self-esteem. Again, this woman may be known as a good thinker, even considered clear headed. But again, she feels she can't trust the insights of others.

This thought "independence" is very confusing for the woman who loves sex addicts. She finds herself in denial about who she really is: she is just another human being with weaknesses and feelings who is not in control of her life. Her need to control her mate, her children, or her work becomes an obsession and she rationalizes that she must use more time and energy to work harder and longer so she can control things better. This thought control issue increases her frustration because she believes her only trustworthy source of insight is herself but her own thinking lands her in the same place time after time. It is a sweet victory for this woman when she can finally begin to trust others to think along with her about herself and her life choices.

Sexually, this woman may also appear to have an independent disposition. The old, "get them before they get you," theme is often a part of the sexual dynamic for this woman. Most sex addicts love and enjoy this type of sexual conduct from a woman. Her conduct gives this woman the illusion that she is choosing to be sexual because she can initiate sex with, and satisfy, her most "experienced" partners. It may even be the foundation upon which her sexuality is built. But there is a price to pay for this illusion.

This woman must often be independent in order to be sexual. She associates independency with being sexually attractive to her partner or partners, when seducing them. But her attitude of wanting sex, "when I want it, the way I want it," is just another form of control. She needs to control her sexual activity because feeling out of control frightens her. She may have a history of sexual abuse or rape, or she may just not be able to trust another person with her emotional and spiritual self. Like the addict, she uses sex to create emotional and spiritual distance, thereby feeling safer.

This form of sexual behavior may, for a while, be physically satisfying. However, eventually this woman longs for intimacy in sex, although she still can't trust enough to be emotionally intimate, for fear of losing control. She doesn't recognize that truly intimate behavior is more than just physical trust. Her boundaries may become rigid and controlling, and she herself may actually be unable to enjoy the sexual encounter she initiates. In extreme cases she may find herself, "not there," during sexual experiences with her partner.

This dependency/independency tension is part of the black and white thinking of women who love sex addicts. These women need to understand the normal stages of dependency, so they can see where they are as individuals and grow into healthier people who don't violate their beliefs and themselves, or feel the need to violate others by the relationship choices they make.

Stages of Dependency

Everyone is born into this world in a state of total dependency. Babies are unable to feed or bathe themselves and are totally dependent upon, and vulnerable to, the whims of those to whom they were born. During this stage, they learn how to manipulate their environment, including those big people in their lives, to meet their inner needs for love and attention, warmth, food, and entertainment. This dependency on family or other caretakers continues. As the child grows, he or she remains dependent for clothes, money for movies, dating, and other aspects of everyday life.

Unfortunately, there are those who never leave this dependency stage. These children may leave home, but recreate the family of origin with friends, lovers or mates. A woman who remains in this stage will still rely on the ability to manipulate those around her to meet her need for self-esteem, acceptance, to feel beautiful, sexual, intelligent. This endless list of needs becomes the responsibility of those she places in the role of "parents" (i.e. lover, friend, husband, boss).

The demand that these needs be met is often presented with an attitude of entitlement, such as you would expect from a child. This woman really believes, "You're supposed to do this for me," or, "You're responsible to meet this need in my life." This woman will often have great difficulty understanding why other people don't put her needs first, and use techniques like guilt, shaming, blaming, pouting, isolation from the person, or tantrums to get her way.

If you are reading this and thinking, "God, I don't do this," ask yourself, "Am I in touch with my real needs, and do I have to ask permission from someone to get these needs met?" If you immediately think of someone from whom you get permission, you are probably stuck in the dependency stage with that person.

When a woman realizes she is in a dependency relationship with a sex addict or other self-picked parents, she may have feelings of anger that she can't think her own thoughts, or meet her own needs, or create her own reality. This can lead to incredible bitterness or resentment.

This reality often hits a woman who is thinking about a separation or divorce. She may tell herself, "I can't leave him," and then list the multiple ways in which she has become totally dependent upon the man. She comes to the same conclusion many children do: "I can't run away." These feelings of being a child in a relationship are painful, but must be faced before she can move into a healthier lifestyle.

Ironically, the dependency stage does have its "pay-offs." The dependent woman always has someone to blame for the fact that her life is empty, devoid of intimacy, or just plain miserable. This stage allows her to blame her sex addict for not taking care of her needs. It also gives her permission never to be responsible for her own needs, or totally responsible for her own behavior. "If he would be _____, then it would be better for me," she tells herself.

This lack of insight into her own feelings, needs or even self-limiting behavior, is symptomatic of a dependency stage woman. She lives by the old childlike delusion of, "My sister made me do it, and therefore I am not in any way responsible for my life." She does so out of fear of making choices that are good for her, and feels she can always look good by blaming the sex addict or other self-picked parent. The reality of her dependency, denial of her own issues, and avoidance of any personal responsibility must be examined by the woman who loves sex addicts—either in a support group or in therapy—if she is ever going to enjoy the freedom of being a responsible adult who is able to choose healthy relationships.

Independency

Healthy children continue to grow until they reach the stage of adolescence. This stage is full of rapid changes in their bodies, in their ability to think, and in their desire for sexual relationships. In this stage childlike behavior becomes subjected to thoughts about abstract things, such as right and wrong. If a child knows when, "that's not fair," it is a good indication that he or she is moving toward independence.

Moving away from mother and father is a good and natural developmental thing that everyone does. Adolescents learn that they can meet some of their own needs, especially when they start making their own money. They want to be treated like adults, though the small amount of money they earn could barely sustain any real lifestyle.

What does this have to do with women who love sex addicts? Many women get stuck in this independent stage of development. They buy, hook line and sinker, our cultural belief that to be totally independent from others is good. They also buy into the belief that, in and of themselves, they should be able to handle all of life's situations, dilemmas, and crises in a calm, cool, and collected manner. Basically, this woman is stuck in the belief that she must be perfect, look perfect and act perfect in all aspects of life. She denies a genuine human need to ask for help, just as a teenager might not admit to needing help from an adult.

This woman may use her sex addict for companionship, a false sense of intimacy (for neither the sex addict nor an independent co-sex addict can allow themselves to be out of control or vulnerable), or just good sex. This woman is certainly troubled by loneliness, and may even fight depression and suicidal thoughts.

Independence has a great price tag on it for the woman who loves a sex addict. She is not allowed to ask for real advice because of her basic mistrust of both others and her environment. This can really be costly when she realizes that she doesn't even trust herself or her own judgments, for fear of being wrong.

Fear is the basic motivation behind an independent woman who loves sex addicts. It is what fuels her need for control of herself, her lover, her relatives, her children, and how others perceive her on a daily basis. This fear affects all of her relationships, especially her marriage. She may appear loving and close, but inside, at her core, she cannot be touched. She is emotionally distant from her mate, even though she may be very sexually active.

She will usually have her own checking account, credit card, and car, and be totally self sufficient. While this may seem healthy, it allows her to pick sex addicts who need her to take care of them emotionally, and often financially. She slowly becomes the mother in the relationship. At this stage she begins to question why she is in this, "disgusting relationship," and may kick him out of the apartment or house that she is paying for.

This woman usually looks "perfect," so others may think of her as not quite human, or somehow better than everyone else, and unapproachable. She would probably not admit that her need to be superior is motivated by fear of being inadequate or unloved.

This woman's apparent strong self-esteem is usually only on the surface, and often is very fragile. It is amazing how some of the most beautiful women feel unattractive, and have a great need to be accepted, even though they deny their need for acceptance and love.

This independent woman may feel good about herself, because she can physically and emotionally get rid of the sex addicts she is attracted to. But she rarely thinks about how she is repeatedly attracted to the same type, or a different level, of sex addict. She loses her boundaries in her next relationship and is off and running again: running from the loneliness, the need to be genuinely loved for who she really is, the need for her fears to be accepted without criticism, the need to move into the last stage of development, which is interdependency. Interdependency will be discussed in the "Solutions" section of the book.

15

Sexuality Issues

Denial of a husband's sexual addiction may just be the tip of the iceberg for the woman who loves sexual addicts. Each woman may have to look into her own "sexual closet" and acknowledge that she was sexually abused as a child or teenager. She will have to look at the possibility that she was molested by a father, brother, uncle, or even a sister, aunt, or mother. It is not uncommon for women who love sex addicts to have had some form of sexual abuse in their own lives.

Sexuality is often a taboo topic, even among the closest of friends. Although our society boasts about its sexual freedom, there is still very little honesty about individual sexuality or sexual history. This silence cannot continue for the woman who loves a sex addict, or recovery will not be possible.

Many of these woman have childhood secrets they promised never to tell anyone, not even themselves. Some, in childhood, took the risk of sharing the secrets, and met with resistance from parents or other adults who did not believe them when they talked about what was really going on in their homes and in their lives. When an authority figure told them, "That could not be true," many of these children believed it was not true. To this day, they continue to deny the reality of their childhood sexual abuse.

If a woman who loves sex addicts wants to recover, she must be willing to look at any area of dysfunction or traumatization of which she has been a victim as a child or adolescent. It is important to recognize what constitutes abuse. It is also important that she not minimize the effects of the abuse she suffered as a child. The following are a few examples of behavior that is sexually abusive to children:

- Having sexual comments directed at you on a regular basis by a significant adult when you were a child.
- Being put in the role of spouse—being a parent's emotional partner. This is called emotional incest.
- Being in an environment where pornography was accessible. Seeing pornography can be as traumatizing to a child as other forms of abuse.
- Being asked to take a shower with Dad or Mom or another adult when you knew you were old enough to do it yourself.
- Being walked in on by father, stepfather, or older brothers while getting dressed.
- Being told women are only good for sex.
- Being made to dress with very little clothing, or clothing covering your entire body.
- Being told your body is shameful.
- Having to watch pornographic videos or watch two adults having sexual intercourse while you were in the same room.
- Having an adult or peer touch your breasts or genitals.
- Having an adult expose their genitals to you.
- Being kissed inappropriately by an adult.
- Being sexually penetrated by an adult or peer without being old enough to give permission.
- Being forced to perform oral sex on an adult.
- Being anally penetrated by an adult or peer.

- Being subjected to an act of incest with a brother or sister.
- Never talking about sex at home, as though it did not exist or it was dirty.
- Being told sex is what bad girls do.
- Having sex as the only topic of conversation in your family.

Sexual abuse can come from strangers, but is more likely to be perpetrated by someone the child knows and trusts. This could be a relative—father, mother, grandparent, older sibling or cousin, aunt or uncle—or a neighbor, family friend, or babysitter. The list of possible abusers, however, is not nearly as long as a comprehensive list of sexually abusive acts would be. The few we have listed here may jog your memory about other incidents in your childhood. *If it feels shameful, it was probably abusive.* If it feels like you should keep it a secret, it was probably abusive. Remember, none of it was your fault.

Some women who love sex addicts can see, at least intellectually, that childhood abuse was not their fault. About their behavior as adults, however, they may feel tremendous shame. They ask themselves, "Why did I do that? Why did I let him do that to me? I should have or could have said no. I'm an adult now. I'm a bad person because that happened." Many thoughts like these will pass through a woman's mind, sometimes to the exclusion of everything else.

The sex addict might even use the woman's past behaviors as a form of blackmail to keep her quiet about what's going on in their relationship. If she threatens to expose him, he might point to her having participated in, or condoned sexually shameful acts in the past. However, each woman must acknowledge all the secrets in her sexual closet if she wishes to heal.

Here is a list of behaviors some women have participated in as adults. You may have more or different ones. The object in looking at past behaviors is not to shame, but to help you identify the problem so you can recover.

- Not ever feeling able to say no to a man who wants to have sex with you.
- Having an affair that your husband does or does not know about.
- Subscribing to pornographic materials yourself.
- Being paid as a nude dancer.
- Being paid for sex in the past.
- Being date raped. "He just kept on going. I could not stop him."
- Being raped by others you may or may not know.
- Having a homosexual experience that you feel shame about.
- Having a problem with masturbation that you keep a secret.
- Feeling like you are a sex addict also.
- Using intoxication as an excuse to act out sexually, or drinking in order to be able to have sex.
- Being videotaped or photographed during sex.
- Having a sexual experience with an animal that you have shame about.
- Being beaten while having sex with a partner.
- Using sex to buy hugs.
- Using sex to fix the sex addict's anger.
- Being sexual so as not to have to carry on a conversation.

- Thinking, "The only way I can get him to stay is to have sex; I have nothing else to offer."
- Being sexual as a gift to the addict, for his birthday or a promotion; not to be intimate but as a tangible gift.
- Having sex with someone you hardly know.
- Participating in mate swapping or group sex at the addict's request.
- Allowing the addict to act out with the children.
- Contracting a sexually transmitted disease.
- Having an abortion because it is what the addict wants.

Perhaps the saddest consequence of all the abuse women who love sex addicts have suffered as children or as adults is the loss of a sense of their own sexuality. When she started her recovery, Julie said her goal was to identify exactly what her sexuality was. She had always let the man in her life decide for her when, and in what way she would express her sexual self. She identified, after awhile, that what she had always thought was being "turned on" was really a response of fear. It was the same feeling she had had as a child being abused.

Women who love sex addicts must be willing to be, as they say in Twelve Step programs, "searching and fearless" in looking at how their sexual selves have been damaged. It may not feel like it at first, but it is really the most loving thing you can do for yourself.

If you are just now identifying childhood or even adult sexual abuse, it will be important for you to have support. The feelings surrounding memories of abuse can be terrifying. For a list of support groups which deal with incest and abuse issues, see the appendix. Do not wait until you get to the Solutions section of the book to begin to heal.

16

Other Defense Mechanisms

How is it that, in spite of all the indicators, a woman who loves a sex addict can live with the relationship as it is? She probably uses a number of other "tools" or coping mechanisms that she has developed over the years. We'll discuss a few of them here.

Disassociation

Disassociation is a clinical term used to indicate a situation where someone is not fully connected with their current reality. It can be as simple as not being present where you are. You are physically present, of course, but mentally and emotionally you have distanced yourself from what's going on around you. Children frequently disassociate as they are being sexually abused, thereby "losing" the memory of what happened to them. When memories of the events return, they are often seen as if on a movie screen.

Adults can disassociate too, and not even be aware that they are doing it. If the events going on around a woman are too painful, she just goes numb. She may stay right where she is, but shut down emotionally. Life becomes a robot-like existence: she goes through the motions but with little or no real involvement with those around her. She may look as if she is listening, but her mind is, "a million miles away." She may feel as if she is wrapped in cotton and can't really touch the people around her. She may literally have no idea what they have said to her.

Disassociation can last for a few moments or for days, weeks, even years at a time. For example, a woman might use disassociation in a sexual situation lasting minutes or hours. One woman, whom we'll call Marie, reported that she regularly disassociated during sex, and would be angry later with her fiance for not having noticed that she wasn't really there. A woman may go through the motions of living for several days, taking care of daily tasks, but with no emotional involvement. Here is a description from one woman:

> I was well into my recovery before I recognized when
> I was disassociating. I would be sitting with people,
> and they would be talking to me, and I would answer
> them, but all the time I was watching the whole scene
> as if from a distance. I could see myself walk and talk,
> and a part of my mind would be saying, "Can't they
> see that I'm not really here?" I would wonder to my-
> self how I could function like that.

One way that disassociation can last for years is in a woman's inability to identify her own experience of current or past emotions. Have you ever gone blank when someone asked you what you are feeling about something now, or something from your past? It can be frustrating when you realize that you can't connect with your own emotions or with your "inner child" in a positive, or even a negative emotional experience.

Disassociation affects the lives of women who love sex addicts in many ways. In the most general of ways, disassociation allows these women to go through life almost as if they live in some kind of fog. They can't seem to connect with what is real around them, and left to themselves, sometimes can't even identify what is real. They may feel like a little lost girl in a strange place, with big people all around, yet they can't find anyone who will nurture them, or help them connect, somewhere to someone or something. They may feel an ongoing ache of separation, yet perform as though they are okay, and nothing bad has ever happened. They tell themselves they will be okay if they can just get connected somewhere.

Disassociation also affects, and is affected by, the woman's relationship with the sex addict. Early in the relationship with the sex addict, she may be impressed with the way the sex addict expresses some of the more extreme emotions like passion, anger, rage, and apparently sincere tears of regret. These moments of intense expression touch something in the woman, allowing her to behave and feel alive for a few moments. She may even set up these sessions so that she can, in a very strange way, feel connected to herself.

She may never understand, when she is doing this, that the unrecovering sex addict can really only feel or express a handful of emotions, and that he often uses these emotions as tools to manipulate his partner into the bedroom, or to stay in a relationship longer than her instincts say she should. The sex addict is an eternal opportunist, and can sense dissociative behavior in his partner, and use it to his advantage. When she is disassociated, she is less likely to object to unwanted sexual advances.

Constant Busyness

Another defense mechanism that helps a co-addict stay comfortable in an uncomfortable situation is constant busyness. Living with a sex addict cannot help but produce strong feelings, and staying constantly busy is a way to avoid those intense feelings. Becky worked 90 hours a week when she was married, so she wouldn't have to be at home and see what was going on in her marriage. When Anne was not at her full time nursing job, she would stay up half the night cleaning, so she could avoid any sexual advances her husband might make. Karen spent hours each day cleaning her house because, as long as she was busy, she didn't have to think about where her husband was and what he was doing. Arlene stayed overly involved in her children's lives in an effort to avoid her spouse. Carla stayed busy with her job and the people she sponsored as a recovering alcoholic. She didn't want to see that her husband was acting out with many of the women in the Alcoholics Anonymous group. These women all used compulsive busyness to avoid feeling their feelings, and to deny the reality of what was going on in their relationships.

Minimization

To minimize something is to make some occurrence or issue smaller than it is in reality. This is the reverse of making a mountain out of molehill; it is making a molehill out of a mountain. The woman who loves sex addicts may use this defense mechanism to avoid her own reasoning or instincts about the sex addict's behavior. She may make statements like these:

- All men do this.
- It's only a phase.
- He needs more excitement than I can give.
- That's the way he grew up.
- The only way he knows I love him is to stick by him.
- What should it matter if I don't know everything he does?
- It could be worse; he could be an alcoholic or drug addict.
- He is such a good mate/husband/father, even though he does this.
- He doesn't beat me.
- He's a good provider.
- He's responsible in other areas.
- He pays the bills regularly.
- He goes to church.
- He helps other people.
- It really doesn't bother me.
- At least he always comes home to me.
- I'm the one he's married to.
- I'm the only one who has ever loved him; what will happen to him if I leave?

Statements of this type allow the women who love sex addicts to focus on at least some positive aspects of their sex addict, almost to the exclusion of his obvious sexually addictive issues and dysfunction. This is like someone saying of the bomb dropped on Hiroshima, "At least it gave jobs to some people," without looking at the death and devastation it caused. This might seem a silly comparison, but many women who love sex addicts do minimize in order to survive the devastation he causes in their lives.

Why? The answer is probably different for each woman. Some women who love sex addicts have come up with these suggestions as to why they minimize the addict's behavior:

- It allows me to stay in the relationship if I don't look at what he is really doing.
- I don't have to feel my real feelings.
- I can avoid my feelings of rejection, abandonment, etc.
- I don't have to deal with how ugly I feel when I'm not in a relationship.
- Even a sex addict relationship is better than no relationship at all, because that would mean nobody loves me.
- I don't have to take responsibility for my issues because I minimize these also.
- I don't have to question my own sexuality or sexual performance if I don't believe that he is getting more satisfaction from masturbation, pornography, other women, or even other men.
- I don't have to shake up my financial and social world.
- If I looked at his issues, I would feel I'm to blame.
- My friends or family told me this would happen and I can't admit they were actually right.
- I can't raise the kids alone.
- I need him for manly tasks and to be a father to our children.
- I would be too embarrassed if anyone really knew what he was doing.
- I can feel safe and loved if I don't believe the truth.
- I can't deal with people finding out I'm not perfect, or that our relationship isn't perfect.

Rationalization

Another deadly defense mechanism for women who love sex addicts is rationalization. This is the ability to make excuses, or come up with logical reasons for the sex addict's behavior or absence. This technique of not looking at the real situation, but creating a reasoning that colors the truth of the matter, is often the topic of recovery group meetings, and recognizing it is sometimes the most painful experience a woman will have in her support group or in therapy.

Most women who love sex addicts rationalized some of their own issues before they even entered their first relationship with a sex addict. This makes it easy to transfer the rationalizing to their new situation. They rationalize, make excuses about the sex addict's behavior, or believe the excuses he gives them, even though they seem far fetched. Here are some examples from recovering women:

- I know he's working late.
- There's nobody there to answer the phone after five but I know he's there.
- This big project is keeping him away.
- The car he is working on is way across town.
- He spends a lot of time shopping for the best price on all the items he buys.
- I'm looking through his wallet for the dry cleaning stubs or a certain credit card. I'm not prying.
- I'm meeting him later just to support him, not to check up on him.

- He has to use his credit cards for business and he charges out-of-town guests on his card locally all the time.
- He has to go to these functions alone because it's strictly business.
- When he gets mad he always drives around for a couple of hours; that's just the way he handles his anger.
- I got this sexually transmitted disease from a toilet seat (even though the gynecologist tells you that's impossible).
- I have to perform oral/anal sex with him to make him happy.
- He is too religious to ever do such a thing.
- He just likes to help people. (But why are they always women?)
- I know she doesn't mean anything to him.
- These long distance charges are on our bill by mistake.
- I'll just bail him out this one time.
- The police are exaggerating his behavior.
- The babysitter must have called these telephone sex numbers when she was here.

Blame

Another defense mechanism that allows a woman who loves a sex addict to stay in denial is blame. She may either blame herself, or blame some outside person or situation for the addict's behavior.

The woman who loves a sex addict, and is blaming herself, is likely to make such statements as, "I know he probably slept with her because I've gained so much weight the last few months," or, "If I'd only been a better wife/lover/mother/mate he wouldn't have done it." Others blame the "other woman," no matter that the rival might really be several other women, or even another man or a child. Julie's first husband acted out with his sister's fourteen year old friend in their living room, while the family was asleep. When he told Julie about it, she confronted the girl he sexually abused, not her own husband, telling the girl never to do that again. This allowed her to deny that her husband had a problem, and allowed her to stay in the marriage.

Another woman, when told by her sex addicted school teacher husband that an 18 year old cheerleader was carrying his baby, blamed the cheerleader for seducing him. Then, like a good wife, she took the girl to the abortion clinic and sat there with her through the whole ordeal.

Some wives blame the boss or the job: "It's not fair of his boss to expect him to entertain those women when they're in town. It's not his fault." Whether a woman blames herself or outside circumstances, she is misplacing the blame. *The addict alone is responsible for his actions and his choices.* As long as she allows herself, or others, to shoulder the addict's responsibilities, she prevents him from feeling the pain that might motivate him to seek help.

It has been said that enabling is murder: if you enable someone to continue any addiction, you are helping him to kill himself. In sexual addiction, and sexual co-addiction, this couldn't be more true. Why then, do women who love sex addicts do it? Why do they deny, minimize, rationalize, become perfectionists, stay busy, blame everyone and everything except the addict and his illness? In a word, fear. Fear is such a great issue for women who love sex addicts that it deserves a section all its own.

17

Fear — The Final Enemy

For the woman who loves sex addicts, fear is often a daily experience. She lives in fear of many things: fear of being alone, fear of being with someone, fear of intimacy (letting someone know who she really is), fear of being hurt, fear of other women, fear of her ability to make healthy decisions, fear of not being able to handle everything, fear of losing the illusion that everything is okay, fear of her past, fear of her future, and more. Let's look at some of these fears individually.

The fear of being alone is one of the biggest fears for many women who love sex addicts. Many of these women have justified some of the most bizarre behaviors or requests of the addict, but also their own tolerance of these behaviors, under the guise of, "Well, at least I'm not alone."

This fear is often repeated by women. They are afraid of being alone or even worse, being alone with their children. "How would I raise them alone?" such a woman might ask. "I'd never make it on my own." These women often fear being alone more than they fear being abused or misused sexually; even more than they fear the grim reality of their children being abused emotionally, physically, or even sexually by the addict.

For many women this fear of being alone is compounded greatly by shame. They may feel shame for being sexually abused, for participating in certain sexual acts with a current or past partner, or for getting pregnant before marriage. They fear what would happen if others found out, so they retreat into a lifestyle of isolation. They fear close relationships like they might fear a surgeon: the fear that people might cut through their masks and see the real pain they carry in themselves is so great that these women stay away from others, and often convince themselves that they are not good enough to be in any decent type of relationship anyway.

Consequently, as these women isolate themselves, they come to depend entirely upon the sex addict for self-esteem, acceptance and anything that even remotely reminds them of being loved.

If he were to leave, the woman's deepest fear of being alone would come true, so she does all she can to make sure that moment never happens. "I'd be so afraid not to be in this relationship, I can't even imagine it," one woman who loves a sex addict said in a meeting.

At the other end of the spectrum are women who fear being involved in a relationship with a man at all. They fear once again finding a prince charming who, after being kissed, turns into a perverted little toad. They are often afraid of the, "here we go again," syndrome. "He looks good but somehow I know it can't last," they may think. They fear being in a relationship with a man because so often their past experiences have confirmed that all men want is sex. They might believe that all men will have affairs outside the relationship, and will eventually leave, so they tell themselves, "I'll be alone anyway, so what's the use?" They would rather be without a relationship than take that risk again.

The fear of being unforgivable or unlovable also plagues women who love sex addicts. This fear is like a very deep shame. A woman who loves sex addicts might, in her bravest moment, acknowledge that what the sex addict does inside or outside the relationship is crazy beyond belief. She might, at times, have even wanted to take part in the sexual acts she has performed within this relationship. No matter what the reason, the woman believes that there is no way she can ever be accepted or loved by anyone else. She believes no one, including God, could forgive her for all the things she has experienced in her relationship with the sex addict. This compounds her need or desire to isolate herself from outsiders.

The fear that someone might discover the reality of her life affects all of this woman's other relationships. Often when a woman is in love with a sex addict, her family and friends begin to ask questions about the relationship, and she finds herself lying, or at least pretending that nothing is wrong. Because she feels she must keep her shameful secret, the woman who loves a sex addict begins to isolate from her family and friends.

"What if they ever found out?" she might think. "What if my husband or mate ever got mad at me and told them what I did with him?" "What if they found his magazines in our house?" "What if he gets arrested for picking up a prostitute or for exposing himself?" "What if he hits on one of my friends?" Or even worse, "What if they find out about what I've been suspecting: that he sexually abuses our children?"

These fears grow and grow over time, until it becomes too difficult for the woman who loves a sex addict to reach out, even to the people who love her.

She may have other fears in the relationship as well. In addition to her fear of leaving the relationship, the woman who loves a sex addict might fear that her partner might give her some type of sexually transmitted disease. She might fear that his pattern will never change, and that she is hopelessly doomed to stay in this relationship. She may fear that she will go crazy if she lives with this fear one more day.

Children are another area chock full of fear for the woman who loves sex addicts. She may fear that the children know that it is not normal for Daddy to beat Mommy and then make love to her right there where the kids can see. She may fear that they will find his videos, magazines, or sex toys. An even greater fear for this woman is fear that they will use these same videos, books, or toys on themselves or on their brothers or sisters, or even on neighbors or extended family members. She may also fear that the children will tell someone in school or in the neighborhood that their Daddy likes other women, or other men for that matter.

The ultimate fear is that her mate is not just sexually abusing her, but that he is sexually abusing her daughters or sons. This fear is usually unspoken, but often very real for a woman who loves a sex addict. It is compounded by the fear that she won't be able to leave, or to protect her children. Such fears can paralyze the emotions, thoughts, and actions of the woman who loves a sex addict.

Charlotte is a woman who was in a relationship with someone she describes as, "a real sex addict." It was hell living with him, she says, but she did, and in the process had two daughters. She was always concerned about him being around the girls, and would protect them. For their sakes, she eventually left the relationship.

Charlotte did not get any help when she left, and soon found herself in another relationship with a sex addict. She married her new "Mr. Wonderful," and they lived two separate lives.

One day her daughter called, crying, scared stiff, and told her mother, "Daddy tried to make me have sex with him." That's when Charlotte realized she had married another sex addict. This one was a lot more discreet about his sexual acting out, and he had progressed in his fantasies and obsessions with the daughter to the point of acting on them.

Fortunately Charlotte's daughter was able to get to a safe place without physical harm, and her call scared the stepfather to the point that he left the home. This story had a happy ending, with all the parties involved getting professional help, but it brings home the reality that some fears may be more legitimate than we care to think.

Another, not so happy story involves a divorced woman who had a ten year old daughter. She began dating a younger man who began to sexually act out with the daughter. They agreed to be "boyfriend and girlfriend." This relationship went on for three years until the daughter and her mother's boyfriend engaged in full intercourse regularly. Finally the girl ran away to live with the boyfriend in another state, and a messy, unhappy legal battle ensued. Cases like this, along with concern about trauma to the child, should be more than enough to cause women who love sex addicts to look at the legitimacy of their fears, and to find the strength to go beyond their fears into a world of safe people who really do want to help.

The fears of women who love sex addicts might best be expressed in their own words. Here are some they have shared with us in support groups:

- I was afraid to stay and I was afraid to leave.
- I was afraid of what he would do to my kids.

- I was afraid I wasn't woman enough for him.
- I was afraid I could never please him sexually.
- I felt like there was something wrong with me.
- I was afraid I couldn't raise my kids by myself.
- I was afraid to let anyone know what was really going on in our lives.
- I was afraid people would tell me I had to stay.
- I was afraid people at church wouldn't understand.
- I was afraid nothing would ever change—that I was doomed, or that it would change and he would leave.
- I was afraid to confront him.
- I was afraid if I changed nobody would like me, including myself.
- I was afraid it was my fault.
- I was afraid I could never find anyone else who would love me.
- I was afraid I was crazy, or would do something crazy.
- I was afraid I would kill him or myself.
- I was afraid he would get arrested.
- I was afraid he would give me some disease.
- I was afraid that he would lose his job.
- I was afraid that he would ask me to do that again.
- I was afraid I couldn't say no if he asked me to do that again.
- I was afraid I was a pervert.
- I was afraid he would tell others what I did.
- I was afraid my friends or family would find out.
- I was afraid he was gay.
- I was afraid that I wouldn't protect my kids if they were being hurt by him.

- I was afraid everything he said was a lie, and that I would believe it.
- I was afraid every man was like this.
- I was afraid that people could see my shame about my life.
- I was afraid my children would tell.
- I was afraid I was only good for sex, and that my sex wasn't ever good enough.
- I was afraid of his anger.
- I was afraid when he came home drunk.
- I was afraid my kids would find his magazines.
- I was afraid my kids would grow up to be sex addicts.
- I am afraid I can't say no when someone I date wants sex.
- I am afraid to share my past with someone new I meet.
- I am afraid this guy will be like all the others; he'll look good at first, then I'll find out he has big problems.
- I am afraid that I'm emotionally or financially dependent on him.
- I am afraid I'll lose the only person who has ever said he loves me.
- I was afraid someone would find the pictures he took of me.
- I was afraid I'd never get better or be able to change.
- I was afraid that he was sleeping with our friends.
- I was always afraid. It seemed like my whole life my decisions were based on one fear or another.

These fears can be overwhelming, and are often depressing. That is why it is so crucial that any woman who is reading this book realize that she must reach out into the recovering community of other women who love sex addicts. She must create a supportive network for herself. Only then will she be able to talk about her fears and hurts, both past and present, and find other loving souls who will be able to listen and identify with her in a very deep and healing manner.

It may seem as if we have focused only on the negative aspects of loving a sex addict. You may find yourself discouraged at this point, and wonder if there is any light at the end of the tunnel. Or, you might be saying to yourself, "I'm not that bad yet. I've never done some of the things they've talked about. I can do this on my own for awhile." You could be vacillating between these two extremes, and be overwhelmed and confused. Or, you might be well on your way to recovery, but experiencing a lack of confidence in yourself and your recovery program.

Look at the chart on the next page. This "valley chart" was composed after many, many interviews with women who love sex addicts, both before and after they began to deal with the problems they experienced as a result of loving a sex addict. Find where you are on the chart. Find the lowest point you may have reached in the past. See how far you have come in recovery. See where you would like to be.

Sexual co-dependency is a progressive disorder. Wherever you are on the down side of the chart, if you continue your old behaviors, you will get worse. If you haven't identified yourself as being near the bottom of the chart, you might want to save yourself the pain of further progression into your disease, and move on to solutions and recovery. The choice is yours.

Recovery from sexual co-dependency is progressive, too. Once you have "hit bottom," and reach out for help, you move to the up side of the chart, and life begins to improve. The more

Recovery Process

Possible childhood sexual trauma

Low self esteem

Need to escape from bad feelings

Development of unhealthy coping skills (control, overeating, constant busyness, etc.)

Getting most self-esteem needs met by relationship

Efforts to control sex addicts behavior

Continued use of unhealthty behaviors to deal with feelings

Romanticizing relationship

Sexually transmitted disease

Isolating from other relationships

Denial of their disease (theirs and others)

Minimizing of violence

Confusion over your reality in relationship

Suicidal ideation or attempt

Despair

Asking for Help or Death

Continued spiritual growth

Increased capacity for interaction

More self-confidence

Continued reliance on Higher Power

New self knowledge

Increased serenity

Healthier relationships

Increasing ability to accept self and others

Dealing with past

Identify and arrest other addictions

Increase self-esteem

Depression lessens

Grieving childhood losses

Reconnect with Higher Power

Sponsor relationships

Beginning of self-care

Start to set boundaries

Beginning to connect with emotional self

Connection with 12 Step group or therapist

Accepting powerlessness over others

Recognizing nature of co-addiction

Identifying destructive behaviors or relationships

effort you put into your recovery, the better your life can become. Again, the choice is yours. Not even the sex addict can keep you from recovering, if that is what you really want. Read on, and you will find that there are "Solutions" to the problem of loving a sex addict that can work for you.

Part III—Solutions

18

Recovery as a Process

There is no one right way to recover from the effects of loving a sex addict. There are many tools available for recovery, and some will work best in one situation, while others will be better in another situation. People differ, too. One woman may use a Twelve Step program as a primary recovery tool. Another will have a strong relationship with a therapist. Many find that a combination of therapy and Twelve Step recovery works for them. It will be important for you to find which tools work for you, and then use them. As you grow and change in your recovery, the tools you use will probably change, too.

Early Recovery

For many women, early recovery still feels like the roller coaster that living with addiction was. New knowledge gained at meetings, from therapists, and from reading materials can cause feelings of relief—"At least now I know I'm not crazy and that this is the real problem," as well as the feeling of despair—"I can't believe I married a sex addict. My life is in a shambles. What if someone finds out?" Many women move in and out of denial in early recovery. Not only do they deny the sex addict's problem, they deny their own part in things, and the effect that living with an addict has on themselves. Many still want to believe that it is all the addict's problem, and that he is the one who needs to change. Early recovery for women who love sex addicts requires that they assimilate a lot of new information. This threatens their view of the world, especially if they are not ready to hear the truth.

Women who are not ready will usually try to control the addict and/or their reactions to him on their own for a while longer. These women need to stay in the denial part of the grief process a little longer. Jane is an example of a woman caught in denial. Jane was married to Max, who had a cross dressing problem all his life. Jane found out about it years into their marriage. They went to get help, and Max kept his problem under cover for seven more years, but eventually he got caught again. Finally, they sought out a therapist familiar with sexual addiction. After months of reading and support groups, marital and individual counseling, Max still chose his addiction, knowing it would cost him his marriage.

Jane was devastated, but she could no longer deny Max's problem. Finally out of denial, recovery for Jane will be a process of reestablishing her life so it can be filled with hope and change for herself. The old saying says, "You can lead a horse to water but you can't make him drink." While it's true that you can't make the sex addict want recovery, you can "take a drink" of recovery for yourself.

For those who are ready, this early recovery time can feel like a life line. One woman said, "I felt like I was drowning, and someone threw me a life preserver." Another one said, "I soaked up all the new information like a sponge. I couldn't read enough." After living with the insanity of sexual addiction, the hours spent in meetings and with a therapist can seem like an oasis of sanity.

The most important part of early recovery is finding hope. Yes, you have identified that there is a problem, and that you have a part in it, but you also learn that there is a solution. The hope of recovery is not necessarily that your marriage will work out, or that the sex addict will get better, but that you can get better. Your happiness will not depend so much on your relationship with others, but on your relationship with your Higher Power and yourself. People and situations may not change, but you can.

Middle Recovery

The willingness to change marks the beginning of the middle phase of recovery. This is the phase where the hard work really begins. You will begin to honestly look at yourself and your reactions. You will work a fourth and fifth step in your Twelve Step group. You will rely more heavily on your higher power. You will begin to set new boundaries with the sex addict. You will receive support from your therapist, sponsor, and other members of your personal support system. You will begin to be able to share your experience, strength, and hope with others new to recovery. As problems arise in your life, you will begin to reach for one of your new recovery behaviors instead of one of your old dysfunctional responses. Life will begin to smooth out.

Recovery is a process, not an event. In the middle stages of recovery you will truly come to believe this. It is in this stage that many co-sex addicts first identify childhood abuse issues. Some women discover other addictions of their own and begin to deal with them: alcoholism, eating disorders, workaholism, and religious addiction are a few. The Twelve Steps, a therapist, and supportive friends will provide the tools you will need to resolve whatever problems your recovery efforts disclose. You will have many, many opportunities to apply the new principles you've learned.

Our culture is very "goal" oriented. We want to know when things will end, and how they will turn out. Our desire to control and eventually "finish" our recovery is great. Reality however, demands that we see our recovery as a lifelong process. Each layer of awareness and feelings you work through will reveal another layer. You may feel defeated by it all, at times. That's a normal reaction but, if you keep coming back, this feeling, too, will pass, and you will find yourself willing and eager for more growth.

Life will always have its ups and downs. There will always be people and events you can't control. Sex addicts will continue to act out. Some sex addicts will begin their own recovery program. You may marry, divorce, have children, or let them go. Indeed, your whole life can change but, through it all, you will be okay because of your own efforts at recovery. There is no one more important or more lovable than you. Treat yourself that way where your recovery is concerned, and you will get better.

Continuing Recovery

Pain is the motivation for most sexual co-dependents, and indeed most human beings, when they first reach out for a solution to their problems. For some time in early and middle recovery, getting back into pain spurs them on to further recovery efforts. Somewhere along the way, they begin to utilize recovery tools as a way to deal with unexpected emotional pain, like the pain they feel when incest memories first surface. Eventually, recovering women who love sex addicts learn that dedication to the principles of recovery can prevent them from getting themselves into painful situations in the first place. They begin to feel empowered to make positive changes in themselves, which are then reflected in the circumstances of their lives. Many even feel grateful for the pain that caused them to reach out for an answer in the first place. Without the problem, they might never have looked for the solution.

While relief from the pain may have motivated these women in the beginning, they eventually reach a point where they use the principles of a recovery program because it brings them joy. As they continue in recovery, they find that they want to share what they've learned with others who are still caught up in the pain of dealing with the sex addict and their reactions to him. In fact, most recovering women find that, unless they share what they've learned, it doesn't last. Without continuous effort it is easy to slip back into old thinking and behavior. Sharing their growth with others reinforces their own recovery.

Time and time again in this book, in meetings, and in working with a therapist, you will experience this process of recovery. It is our hope that the following chapters will give you some sense of what you can expect.

19

Developmental Recovery: From Dependency to Interdependency

One way to look at recovery is to view it as a journey from dependency to interdependency. Such a journey parallels a normal maturing process. Many women who love sex addicts experienced limited emotional growth as children and teenagers, and will, instead, experience this growth as part of their recovery process. You may have identified that you are sometimes stuck in dependency or independency when we described them in the "Similarities" section. Interdependency is the final stage of human development, and even for women who love sex addicts, it is possible.

Interdependency is so uncommon in our culture that it may appear odd to some. This might be due to the fact that most of our American adult relationships appear to be primarily controlling/dependency relationships, or independent relationships.

This last stage of development in the human process ideally occurs somewhere between our early to late twenties and death. This is the stage where the young adult raised in a normal family realizes, "Maybe Mom and Dad weren't so stupid after all." Or, for those who recognize the severe dysfunction in their family of origin, it is a place where they can begin to make their own choices about what is best for them in their lives. This is the stage where the recovering woman is able to ask to be hugged by her parents and siblings, or by other trusted people if her family is still unsafe. This is a place where it is okay, and not shameful, to not know all the answers. It's even okay to make mistakes. This is a stage where the recovering woman really can come to believe that she is loved by her parents and friends for who she is, and not for what she does. Realizing this brings much comfort for the insecure child in the adult body.

It sounds wonderful to be able to trust a major caregiver; not to be criticized for being human, no matter what you've done; to be able to sincerely ask if you are loved by someone, and to have them smile back at you and reassure you that you are loved. It sounds wonderful to be able to trust others and to be trusted; to be able to help others and know that helpfulness is received and appreciated; to be able to be ourselves and for others to be themselves, with no need to control each other. Ultimately, it feels wonderful to be vulnerable with someone, and to have him or her be vulnerable with you. This is called intimacy, and it is wonderful.

The interdependency stage allows others to have their needs, boundaries, and defects of character. It also gives you permission to have your needs, boundaries, and defects of character. Because many people have a dysfunctional parenting history, this stage is not normally reached in our society, but it is still possible to achieve.

It can be a scary thing to enter this stage of development, but interdependency is a stage where you are able to have the freedom to love and accept yourself and others. In this stage, respect is restored and trust in the important support people in your life becomes possible. Honesty, unconditional love and concern, individual integrity, and respect become a reality in real and special enduring relationships.

This is the stage where the child who depended totally upon mom and dad, and then became independent, is now able to return home as an adult to other adults. This is the stage where each of us becomes willing to accept our own humanness, strengths, and defects of character, and to accept these qualities in others. We begin to trust people with our selves.

This may be the hardest stage of all for women who love sex addicts to achieve in this independent/dependent culture. Unlike other stages, interdependency is, at best, difficult for people who come from dysfunctional families. If you have always lived by the, "don't talk, don't trust, don't feel," rules, you will be challenged at your core to push through to this stage of truth and intimacy. The process can be further complicated if you believe that you must be perfect, and capable of handling all of life alone. If you hold on to these old ideas, you will not come to the point of trusting your own human frailties and weaknesses to other frail creatures who, being human, might let you down.

You may wonder, then, how you can reach this stage of interdependency, when you may be a dependent or independent type of woman who loves sex addicts. Reaching this stage minimally requires that those who come from dysfunctional families, or who are acting out addictions in any way, begin a recovery process. This process requires honesty with yourself, and participation in a Twelve Step program that can become an integrated lifestyle of recovery. For some, pushing through to this stage may also require help from a caring professional who is able to act as a guide to interdependency. More will be said later about choosing a professional therapist.

This stage of development is probably not possible in a relationship if either partner is unwilling to look at him or herself, and actively pursue a recovering lifestyle. Knowing this crucial truth can cause you to question and/or rearrange your current relationships so that you can, in recovery, experience the safety of being yourself with others, without a need to act out any of your issues with a sex addict.

20

Feelings in Recovery: Reconnecting With Your Emotional Self

One of the first realities the woman who loves sex addicts hits when she comes into recovery is her feelings. "Keep coming back," she'll be told in Twelve Step meetings, "and you'll feel better." If you hear laughter following that statement from group members, it is probably because they remember only too well when they worked through the shock and denial of pre-recovery days, and first allowed themselves to experience emotions they'd been stuffing for years. What you may discover is that before you feel better, you just feel MORE.

At first, the vague nebulous pains or weird feelings inside can be confusing. The initial feelings may be closely related to the shock of the grief process discussed in Chapter 13. You may experience a sort of numbness: "I can't believe it," you will hear yourself, and others, say at meetings. The shock stage feels a little like disassociation, when you are disconnected from your emotional self. Just as in an abusive situation, what you are experiencing may be so foreign to you that you just blank out any feelings about it.

Shock does not happen just once in recovery. You might experience it first when you find out that your husband is a sex addict. You might feel it again when you look back over your life and see that many men you've been involved with were sex addicts of one kind or another. You could very well go into shock if you discover that you've been infected with a sexually transmitted disease as a result of his acting out, or when you discover that your children have been abused by a sex addict. Later, in recovery, you might re-enter this shock phase if you discover sexual abuse from your own childhood. Shock is common. It is normal. Like denial, it helps you survive an emotionally overpowering situation, and gives you time to regroup and begin to assimilate this new information you've been presented with.

The next feeling many women feel in recovery is ANGER. They feel angry about many things. They can be angry at their spouse for acting out, angry at themselves for not identifying the problem earlier, angry at God for allowing this to happen, and angry at life for not being perfect.

Anger toward a mate or lover is, for some women, the strongest part of the initial anger they feel. It is easy to look at his shortcomings: affairs, pornography, masturbation, and so forth. It is much harder to look at her own shortcomings. Sooner or later, it dawns on her that the series of mates she's had, or her husband, may not be the only ones who have the problem. It may be the woman herself. This realization may come when a friend or relative asks, "Why do you always seem to pick these types of guys anyway?" Her face may flush, her fists clench, and later her tears may roll. She will ask herself, "Why DO I pick these guys?", and turn the anger back on herself.

WHY? WHY? WHY? This question may lurk constantly in the back of your mind when you begin the recovery process. You will naturally come up with many rationalizations as to why you deserved your relationships. Maybe you believe it's because you were sexually abused. Maybe you believe you're not worth anything better, or that all you're good for is sex. You may feel angry at yourself for being too fat, or skinny, or stupid, or ugly, and believe you have to take what you can get.

"Could it have been that premarital sex I had with my husband?" you may ask yourself. "Am I being punished for that? If I hadn't let him do that to me he would never have seen me as cheap and treated me this way. Maybe this is happening to me because I was raped as a child or adolescent, or even as an adult. Maybe I've always been a victim in relationships. Perhaps, because of my past nobody else will want me. Maybe I just shouldn't be too picky."

The list of possibilities goes on and on, but the truth is that sex addicts, and perpetrators of sexual abuse or sexual crimes, generally have an uncanny ability to pick up on a woman who has been emotionally deprived, or who has low self esteem. They seem to know when a woman has been a victim of sexual trauma before. They can see the emotional scars in her eyes or in her spirit. The "Don't hurt me" sign over her head reads, "Available to hurt," to a sex addict. Although this might be hard to understand, many women who have been interviewed in rape crisis centers or sexual abuse units describe similar scenarios, which have happened to them more than one time. It is not her fault that the perpetrator or sex addict can sense her vulnerability. To him it's like blood to a hawk.

It may be very hard to read this right now if you are having bad memories or flashbacks about times you have been violated. You will be okay. If you have a significant other, or support group, be honest with them about what really happened, and how you feel about it. You might feel tremendous hurt, shame, or anger, but you can survive these strong feelings. Remember, reliving the situation cannot kill you; trying to deny the feelings surrounding your abuse can.

For many women in recovery, simply identifying these feelings can be difficult—perhaps even more difficult than feeling them. Another hurdle many women must overcome is their inability to trust others with the feelings they do identify. It may be helpful to look at dealing with your feelings as a process.

First, give yourself permission to feel. Try not to automatically shut down by eating, drinking or shopping those feelings away. Be still enough, long enough, to allow your feelings to surface.

Next, give yourself permission to be honest about what you feel. Some of the feelings you will have in recovery, or in everyday life, are not pretty. You still need to be honest about them if you wish to grow. Can you allow yourself to acknowledge when you feel hate, anger, fear, resentment, worthlessness, a terrific need to control? If you find it difficult, it may help to remember that feelings are best resolved when they are not labelled as good or bad.

Third, begin to identify exactly what your feelings are. Most feelings can be categorized into one of five areas: sad, mad, glad, scared, or ashamed. Try those on for size, and see if what you are feeling fits one of those categories.

If you are still having trouble identifying your feelings, a Feeling Exercise might be in order. Look at the feeling list in Appendix A. Write down the first ten feelings that jump out at you. Next, write the following sentences for each of the feelings you chose:

1. I feel (put feeling word here) when (put a present situation when you feel this).

2. I first remember feeling (put the same feeling word here) when (explain earliest occurrence of this feeling).

For example, take the word "frightened." You might write, "I feel frightened because my husband is late tonight, and that usually means he's acting out. I first remember feeling frightened like this when my daddy would come home late from work. Mom was always upset, and really took it out on us kids. Then Daddy would come home, and they would have a big fight, and we would really be scared then, because Daddy always threatened to leave and never come back."

After you have written your sentences out, find a safe person to share them with, such as a sponsor or therapist. After several such exercises, you will be able to identify your feelings more readily, and will find it easier and easier to share them with a safe friend.

Wait a minute. Are we telling you to talk about feelings? You bet. Part of the rules in dysfunctional families read, "don't talk, don't trust, don't feel." In order to really heal, you will need to break every one of those rules. You will need to combat those old misbeliefs, and others. You might think, "If I share these feelings, I'll be overwhelmed, and I won't know what to do." You might believe that your feelings are too unimportant to bother anybody with, or that what's happened to you, and your feelings about it, are not as bad as everybody else's. Remember, you gave yourself permission earlier to talk. It is essential to your healing.

We cannot stress too much that the person you share your feelings in recovery with should be someone you feel safe with. Your spouse is probably not the person you will feel safest with, especially if he is not in recovery. Your parents are not likely to understand either, unless they are working a recovery program. A safe person might be a therapist, minister, sponsor, or close friend who understands your need to let go of these feelings.

Strong feelings, such as anger and depression, are a normal part of the process of grief over the painful reality of loving a sex addict. In fact, these feelings can motivate you to further efforts at recovery, as is illustrated by the story of a woman we'll call Angela. Angela was a sixteen year old girl with an I.Q. of 133. She was smart, creative, and witty, but she was sexually abused several times by both men and women. When she went into treatment she did not really want to focus on her sexual abuse issues. Shortly after leaving the hospital she ran away from home, and was picked up by a cab driver who took her home and raped her. After that incident, she felt angry enough to work on the obvious cycle of victimization in her life.

Another person, Kelly, was sexually abused by a family member at age five, and again at age thirteen. In her adolescence she was physically forced to perform oral sex, and she was also gang raped.

Kelly eventually found herself in an in-patient psychiatric hospital for depression and anxiety. She had become unable to function in her normal roles as employee, mother, and wife. Her inner life was full of these abuse and rape experiences. She was having flashbacks to these experiences on a daily basis. She numbed these memories the best she could with alcohol and prescription drugs.

During her treatment Kelly did well for about a week. After that, she began to shut down emotionally and just pretended that she was doing better. Upon discharge, Kelly agreed to out-patient treatment twice a week, but she didn't stop using alcohol and prescription drugs. One night, she went out with a female friend and got drunk. A sex addict hit on her at the bar. He took her to her girlfriend's house and raped her.

Kelly was infuriated at herself for letting this happen again. She was so angry that she said, "Whatever I have to do to stop this, I'm ready to do it." She started again on a path of recovery, and now no longer allows herself to be abused by anyone.

Many women who love sex addicts have great difficulty expressing anger towards their abusers, or towards their sex addict partners. It takes time in recovery, and support from others, to face this fear of expressing anger at people who have had power over them in the past. It may be necessary for these women to start small, and work up to larger issues. Practicing with a sponsor before confronting a spouse can be helpful. Since these women have had little role modeling in appropriate expression of anger, it is easy for them to overdo it or under-do it in the beginning. They, and you, have a right to healthy expression of anger, though.

The anger you feel towards yourself and others can put you back into shame, and perpetuate your acting out patterns, or it can motivate you to further recovery. We hope that Angela's and Kelly's experiences in dealing with strong feelings will inspire you to begin to deal with yours as they surface.

21

Grieving Losses

We have talked a lot about the grief process in general, but what do we mean by grieving losses? What has a woman lost as a result of living with and loving a sex addict? The answers to these questions will vary from person to person, and from story to story, but everyone suffers losses in a sex addict/co-addict relationship.

Many of the things you are asked to do in recovery are both necessary and difficult. The only thing that would probably be harder would be not to recover at all. Identifying and grieving losses is one of the most intense experiences in recovery. Even as authors, writing about losses feels sad. As we share the stories of these women who have been so open with us, we feel some of their pain, and it triggers some of our own pain. Thankfully, by this point we have learned that we can survive pain, if we share what we are feeling with others in recovery. We want you to know that we recognize that this may be difficult for you; we also want you to know that we believe in your ability to work through your sometimes devastating losses.

We asked the women we interviewed to share with us some of the losses they felt as a result of identifying and dealing with having loved a sex addict. For most of them, it meant going back to childhood to see just where the initial damage was done. Several of the women identified these losses as they worked on their Fourth Step inventory in their Twelve Step program. Some did this grief work with a therapist. All those we talked to found this emotionally draining experience to be necessary to their continued healing.

The initial experience of loss for many, many women occurred in their family of origin, either through neglect or abuse. In her story, Marie recognized a feeling of loss as a big part of her childhood: loss of power, loss of love, loss of protection, loss of herself. Julie identified the loss of her ability to experience the normal development of her sexuality. Most abused children endured a loss of their reality when the adults around them denied that what they suffered was abuse. If you grew up in a dysfunctional family, you missed out on appropriate levels of nurturing in a number of areas: emotional, physical, mental, and spiritual. What areas stand out for you? You may want to take a few minutes to really consider what losses you've suffered.

As these women grew into adults, the losses continued. Every time they allowed their boundaries to be violated they suffered another loss. Every time they said yes when they really wanted to say no, they lost a little piece of themselves. Every time they denied their reality, or someone denied it for them, there was a loss. For these women and perhaps for you, losses like these happened hundreds of times a day.

Some losses were more major. What about the loss of years of productivity due to depression? What about financial losses as a result of the addict spending money on pornography or prostitutes? Did you miss any time at work due to physical illness—perhaps from a sexually transmitted disease? Did you have an abortion because the addict wanted it? Did you lose friends because the addict acted out with them, or insisted you not see them again? Did you pass up chances to improve your own life because the addict needed you for some reason? Marie gave up her hopes for college. So did Julie. Have you missed out on your children's formative years because you were so obsessed with what was going on with the addict? Or, like Becky, were you so cut off from your feelings, and what was going on around you, that you missed entire years of your childhood?

Other losses are less obvious. There is the loss of the dream you had for your life. There is the loss of your integrity, and your value, and your specialness. In a meeting, one woman said, "It's so awful to realize that I could have been any woman, and it would have been okay with him. He had another woman in his life so fast it made my head spin. It didn't matter that it was me he was having sex with. I felt so insignificant when I realized that. It was almost as if my existence didn't matter at all. And I gave my whole life to that man."

Perhaps the most overwhelming losses have to do with your sexuality. In many cases, women who love sex addicts lost the right to discover and develop their own sexuality. They lose the right to their own bodies. They lose the right to say no. They lose the right to feel sexual feelings in a healthy way. They lose their virginity, and also their ability to feel even remotely good about being sexual beings. They lose the right to have joy as part of their sexual experiences.

You will be able to come up with a list of your own losses. Extreme sadness and depression are common feelings that everyone experiences as they identify the devastating losses they've had in their lives. You may feel overwhelmed as you begin to recognize your losses, but there is hope as you work to recover from them.

What is the best way to handle the emotions that come up as you grieve your losses? You may find it necessary to keep in touch on a daily, or even hourly, basis with a sponsor or other supportive person. Get professional help immediately if you experience suicidal thoughts or impulses as you work through the pain. Remember, you don't have to do any of this alone. Lean heavily on your Higher Power, and allow yourself to feel as you walk through your personal journey of recovery.

Anger and sadness are the primary emotions that will surface as you identify your losses. If you find a safe environment, you can express these feelings in a healthy, non-destructive way. Some women find that pounding the sofa cushions with a tennis racket can help relieve anger. One woman said she found pulling weeds, and pretending it was her husband's hair, helped her. Shadow boxing, screaming, stomping, kicking a teddy bear across the room, and crying are all ways to express anger. Talking about your feelings helps. Writing in a journal relieves intense feelings for some people. Writing letters you may or may not ever send works for some. If you don't know what to do with your feelings, ask someone for help. Don't just stuff them again. You are worth recovering, and worth listening to.

The following is a writing exercise, originally presented in a workshop by Virginia Nelson, M.A., that we have found to be helpful. It will be published in her upcoming book, *From the Ashes of Dreams: Growth and Reality.* It is reprinted here with her permission.

On The Way To Healing by Virginia Nelson, M.A.

Many of my clients have asked me to write down some of the exercises I give as homework for healing—so here they are with love.

1. Start your own journal—write your thoughts and concerns, then put the journal in a safe place. It is your journal to write in as you choose. It is wonderful to re-read from time to time to measure how far you have come.

2. To calm down quickly, do the following deep breathing exercise:

   Breathe in through your nose slowly to the count of seven (filling all the way down so your abdomen rises).

   Hold for a count of one—exhale through your mouth to the count of seven, then puff, puff, puff so that your chest sinks towards your lower abdomen—then breathe in slowly through your nose once and out rapidly—return to normal breathing.

3. Cleansing Exercises—for Anger, Rage, Hurt and Grief: It is important you do this *whole* exercise at the same *time*; do not leave out parts of it.

   - Write: How dare you (insert name and write whatever is appropriate). Do this as many times as necessary. Pound a pillow if you need to.
   - Write as many times as necessary (insert their name) I hurt because you_____ (complete sentence). Cry if you need to.
   - Shower and wash your hair—let the water pour over you, dry off, put on something comfortable.
   - Do the deep breathing exercises.
   - Now, to complete your exercises, write: I am now okay because_____

   _____

And/or I am doing well because and/or I am
succeeding in healing because _____

_____

Your anger and hurt will dissolve as you repeat this exercise as many times as you need to.

4. To calm your emotions, the following exercise often helps.
The emotions are like water. This exercise takes 20 to 30
minutes.

- Sit upright comfortably, feet flat on the floor or on a
  stool, arms relaxed in your lap.
- Do the deep breathing exercise.
- Visualize a storm on a lake; the water is very rough.
  You are in a small boat; the sun is behind the clouds.
- Now see and feel the wind calming down the waves,
  getting less wild.
- Watch as the waves become ripples, the winds turn to a
  breeze, the sun comes slowly out from behind the
  clouds.
- The sun is out, the water is calm. Breathe in deeply.
  Smell the clean air.
- The sun begins to set; feel the warmth of the sun,
  experience the light from the sun, know God's love is in
  the light and warmth—breathe it in.
- Watch as the golden sun sets on the horizon, turning
  the lake into shimmering gold.
- The sky is deep blue-purple, the horizon is golden, the
  lake is shimmering gold—let go of all tension; sit in the
  boat at total peace, in harmony with the golden water.

As the sun sinks deeper and deeper, lower and lower, you remain calm and tranquil.

- Now as you feel ready, return to where you are, feeling at peace and in harmony, to proceed with your day refreshed. Remember you can go back to the lake anytime.

5. You must claim your victory before it happens—so visualize yourself as you want to be, doing what you want to be doing. Hear what people are saying, feel how good you feel. Do this before getting out of bed, before going to sleep at night, and several times during the day. Claim it now!

Grieving losses in recovery is a process. It is something that is done over time, often in bits and pieces. As you grow in recovery, and more of your past comes into your conscious awareness, you will find that you have new things to grieve. Don't give up. You will survive. There is light at the end of the tunnel. Soon you will be helping others to work through their feelings and move on to healthier behaviors.

22

Restructuring Sexual Boundaries

Having sexual boundaries may be a foreign concept for women who love sex addicts. A boundary can be defined as the place where you end and another person begins. This sounds simple enough, but in the context of a relationship with a sex addict, who feels he is to have absolute, 110% right over his partner's body, and she is to have little if any boundaries of her own, confusion is inevitable.

Apart from what they learned in their family of origin, or from the media, many women who love sex addicts have no idea about sexuality, much less setting sexual boundaries. This is another area of recovery that is both difficult and crucial, and one most women who love sex addicts know so little about. Let's start with some common definitions of different types of sex, before we talk about establishing boundaries.

Personable Sex: Both partners enjoy each other as a person, and are able to communicate sexual needs to one another. One or both partners may or may not have an orgasm, but both have a sense of nurturing each other. Sex is not the focus or the priority in this relationship.

Physical Sex: This is where one or both partners enjoy primarily the physical act, but still the relationship is not threatened. This type of sex may happen to all couples eventually. There's not much feeling, but no shame either.

Objectifying Sex: This type of sex may or may not be pleasurable to one partner, but the other one is fantasizing about other acts with this same partner while in one position with this partner. One person's orgasm is the focus of this sexual act. The other partner may or may not feel that they are important to the orgasmic partner.

Masturbating Sex: One partner is fantasizing about other partners, porno movies, books, or someone of the same sex, while having sex with his partner. The fantasy is the excitement that leads to the person of focus having an orgasm, not his partner. The partner may feel used, absent, or resentful of this sexual encounter.

Violating Sex: This is where one partner demands from his partner certain behaviors. She does not feel comfortable in doing them, but she complies, hoping he will stop nagging her for this sexual act. The partner feels violated as a person, and may have anger or resentment toward her partner for insisting that they do this activity.

Traumatizing Sex: The partner is forced physically, or with the threat of a weapon or physical pain, to perform a sexual act with her partner. This constitutes rape, and the woman may feel incredible fear of the perpetrator, as well as feelings of victimization and trauma.

You may have experienced more than one type of sex with your partner or partners. You hear story after story of "how great the sex was until we moved in together or got married." A highly skilled sex addict will usually start off early in the relationship with socially acceptable sex, and then progress to any other level of sexual behavior that his disposition allows. But what about boundaries? Here is where you will need a support group to help you, especially if you feel you are in a situation that is violating or traumatizing to you. The rationale that you deserved what happened to you must be thoroughly confronted and dealt with before you can establish sexual boundaries.

Once you have a sense of worth, and believe that you have the freedom to choose the type of sex you will have, and with whom you will be sexual, you will have to evaluate your current relationships. To evaluate the type of sexual relationship you are experiencing, ask yourself questions like these:

- Is he safe for me to remain sexually open or active with? Is he acting out with other partners? What are the chances of my getting a sexually transmitted disease?
- Am I willing to recruit a support group to help me keep the boundaries that I establish for myself? (Remember

that being alone is how most women who love sex addicts got where they are today.)

- Am I willing to seek professional help to facilitate my own personal growth, so as not to allow further violation of my sexuality?
- Is my partner willing to be honest with himself and with me? Is he able to tell me what is going on in his head when we are being sexual together?
- Is my partner willing to seek professional help to facilitate his personal growth, and to arrest his addiction?

Once you choose the type of sex you desire for yourself, you are responsible to keep that boundary intact. If you choose not to have sex with a particular person, or simply choose to have sex only when you feel it is okay with you, then you're responsible for speaking up if your sexual boundaries are infringed upon. A note of caution must be made to anyone starting out for the first time on this boundary business: You must have a strong support group, have agreed upon consequences by both partners when boundaries are violated, and make your sexual boundaries clear early in the relationship, before the sexual act. It is much easier to maintain a boundary you have discussed with your partner prior to getting into bed.

For example, if you've been having flashbacks to childhood sexual abuse of a certain kind—say oral sex—you might feel uncomfortable with that particular form of sex. It will be easier for you to maintain your boundary about not having oral sex if you discuss it with your partner before you get into bed and you both get caught up in the moment. You might not feel as comfortable saying no when you think he might be disappointed or angry with you, so you are more likely to run the risk of doing something that will make you feel bad about yourself.

A marital therapist might be helpful in working out boundaries that are agreeable to both partners. In addition, you should find at least one safe person with whom you can discuss sex, other than your partner. This could be a therapist, but probably a Twelve Step sponsor would be more readily available to help you process the feelings that are sure to accompany your trying these new behaviors. Always remember that it took a long time to get sick, and it will take a while to get well. You don't have to be perfect, but you owe it to yourself to be persistent. Eventually, you can be comfortable setting and maintaining new sexual boundaries.

A special note to incest survivors and other sexual trauma survivors: as you begin to process memories of prior abuse, you may find that sexual acts you could tolerate before become impossible to endure. You may identify a strong aversion, or just an uneasy feeling about a particular behavior. Allow yourself to say no, or even to stop in the middle of sex, if you need to. Your partner may not understand or approve, but you need to listen to that inner voice, and act in your own best interest. If both you and your partner can talk about what is going on, the relationship can survive while you heal old wounds. If you ignore that little voice, you are perpetuating a pattern of abuse. You deserve so much more than that.

23

Twelve Step Support Groups

Some women who love sex addicts discover their sexual co-dependency after they have been in recovery in one Twelve Step program or another for several years. You may already be familiar with Twelve Step recovery. However, a good number of women are introduced to the Twelve Step philosophy after they identify one, or several, sex addicts in their lives. For those who have no experience with Twelve Step programs, a brief history is in order.

The original Twelve Step group was Alcoholics Anonymous, which was first organized in 1935. AA is a program of spiritual recovery, which offers fellowship with, and guidance from, other recovering alcoholics. In the fifty-five years since AA was founded, many other fellowships were formed, based on the same twelve steps and the principles they embody. Narcotics Anonymous, Gamblers Anonymous, and Overeaters Anonymous are examples. Twelve Step groups for family members were developed as well. These include Al-Anon Family Groups for friends and family members of alcoholics, Nar-Anon and Gam-Anon for friends and family members of drug addicts and compulsive gamblers, respectively.

In the area of sexual addiction and sexual co-addiction, the Twelve Step philosophy has been found, not surprisingly, to be an extremely effective tool for recovery. Sex Addicts Anonymous, Sexaholics Anonymous, and Sex and Love Addicts Anonymous meetings are growing in number daily. Co-SA (Co-dependents of Sex Addicts) and Co-SLAA, the counterpart meetings for family members, are the twelve step meetings most likely to be helpful to the readers of this book. In addition, Incest Survivors Anonymous groups will be helpful to the co-sex addict who is a survivor of childhood sexual abuse.

Choosing A Group

Co-SA and Co-SLAA groups have been established in some metropolitan areas for several years. In other areas of the country they may be hard to find. You can check with your local Council on Alcohol and Drug Abuse—they usually maintain lists of local Twelve Step meetings. Another place to check would be your mental health association. In some communities, the United Way office can point you in the right direction. If you are unable to locate a meeting, contact one of the resources listed in the appendix at the end of the book. Don't give up. You need the support you will find there. You deserve to heal.

When you do find a group, plan to attend at least six meetings before you make a decision about whether you think it will be helpful to you. It can be frightening in the beginning, especially if the sexual addiction has been kept a secret. You may feel shame that you are even considering attending a meeting that might label your partner a sex addict. If your partner is not yet in recovery, you can expect resistance to your attending any meetings at all. It might be something you wish to keep to yourself for awhile. You can share your concerns with others in the group. They will understand. Whatever your problems, there will be someone there who has experienced something similar.

Perhaps you will attend your first meeting at the suggestion of a therapist, or because your spouse has gone into treatment, or started attending SAA or SLAA meetings. You may feel that there is nothing wrong with you, and that everything would be fine if only he would change. Many women believe that it is only the sex addict's problem. Whatever you believe in the beginning, keep an open mind. It is impossible to live with a sex addict and not be affected in some way. If he gets help he will get better, but his recovery won't necessarily have any affect on what may be wrong with you.

It is important to give Twelve Step recovery a chance. It is different than working with a therapist. The women in the Co-SA meetings are peers. They have lived with the problem of sexual addiction, and used the steps and principles of the program to recover from its effects in their lives. They will not judge you, or tell you what to do. They will offer their experience, strength, and hope. They will tell you what worked for them. They will love and support you no matter what is going on in your life. Reaching out for their support is essential to the healing process. Sexual addiction and co-sexual addiction are diseases that promote shame and isolation. These diseases are not something you can handle on your own. If you could, you would have done so already. Many women find themselves stuck trying to handle it on their own with no way out. Finding a Twelve Step support group, and working the Twelve Steps in your life, are important parts of finding your way out of the pain.

Program Tools

The new ways of thinking and behaving you discover in Twelve Step recovery have been likened to a set of tools. Women who love sex addicts are used to responding to life with the "tools" they learned to use in childhood. Most often, these childhood responses are not appropriate for adult situations, and certainly don't work very well if you're living with a sex addict. You need a new set of tools, designed to help you not only survive, but grow, whether the sex addict is in recovery or not. What are these tools in Twelve Step recovery?

The Telephone

The first tool many women in recovery are encouraged to use is the telephone. At most meetings you will find a phone list of members to call between meetings when things get tough. If you aren't offered a phone list, ask for one, or ask a few members to share their phone numbers with you. Then use them. Women who love sex addicts are pros at putting themselves last. You might think, "I'll be bothering her. She's probably right in the middle of dinner. It's too early. It's too late. What if she's in the bathroom?" Don't let these thoughts keep you from reaching out.

Part of being a woman who loves a sex addict is isolation. If you are to recover, you need to stop isolating and let somebody know what you're thinking and feeling. Often that phone call will prevent you from acting out your old behavior with the sex addict and perpetuating the dysfunction in your home. The sooner and more often you reach out, the easier it will become. One woman's sponsor suggested she make "practice calls." She told her to call when things were going okay and say, "This is a fire drill." When crisis did come along, it was easier for this young woman to reach out with the telephone and get the support she needed.

The Slogans and The Serenity Prayer

Another program tool that is easy to latch on to in early recovery is the use of what are called "the Slogans," and the Serenity Prayer. The slogans can vary a little from one recovery program to another, but there are several that work well for women who love sex addicts.

One Day at a Time

Fear about the future, and shame over what has gone on in the past, may overwhelm a woman when she is living with sexual addiction. She may want guarantees that the pain she is in won't last forever. When things are going well, she may fear that disaster lurks just around the corner. She spends much time and energy trying to insure that the future will be either the same or different. She fears that nothing will ever change, and she fears that it will all change, and she won't know how to handle it. She spends a lot of time "what if-ing": what if he leaves me? what if I say no to him? what if someone finds out about his behavior? what if someone finds out about my behavior? Her fears can be endless.

Taking one day at a time can relieve these fears. You truly have no control over what happens tomorrow. You do have control over your responses to what faces you today. In this moment, are you safe from harm? If not, you can take steps to be safe. If you are not in any danger right this minute, you can relax and turn your thoughts to what is in front of you to do. Worrying about tomorrow is unlikely to have any positive effect on future events anyway. Your energy is better spent taking care of today's problems today, or enjoying today's lack of problems by relaxing your usual tight grip on events in your life.

You may feel compelled to take action, to "do something," about everything that happens in your life, the moment it happens. The slogan, "One Day at a Time," is a reminder that not everything can or even should be handled today. It is often better to wait until your churning emotions have had a chance to settle down before you make any decision. As hard as it is, you may realize in recovery that what you need to do today is just feel your feelings, and not take any action at all. When you are in the midst of intense feelings, this slogan reminds you that nothing lasts forever, and that tomorrow can be different.

"One Day at a Time," is also a reminder that we cannot change what has gone on in the past. Dwelling on past injustices is hurtful and is not likely to produce the kind of growth you need. It is more likely to produce shame, anger, and fear. While acknowledging your past is important, you often poison what could be a beautiful today by constantly reminding yourself of how awful your past has been. One therapist recommended that her clients, "keep your minds where you bodies are," in order to stay out of yesterday and tomorrow. It takes practice, but it can be done when we try to take just One Day at a Time.

Live and Let Live

For many women who love sex addicts, living a life of their own is a totally foreign idea. They have based their identity for so long on the sex addict in their lives, or on their children, or their parents, or their jobs, that developing a life of their own can seem terrifying. This slogan reminds the woman who loves sex addicts that her first responsibility is to live her own life. She is an important part of a higher plan, or she wouldn't be here. Her life has purpose and meaning, independent of her usefulness to other people.

This one word, *"live,"* carries with it the message that you alone are responsible for the quality of your life. It is not up to the sex addict or anyone else to make you feel happy or fulfilled. This awareness of responsibility does not feel good to most newcomers, but over time you will develop a real sense of freedom and empowerment as you see where you have given control over your thoughts, emotions and your very life to the sex addict. If you are to have any serenity, you must take your life back and begin to live from your own set of values.

The rest of this slogan—and let live—requires that you stop trying to control the lives of those around you, particularly the sex addict. From childhood on, many women who love sex addicts have felt, or were even told, that they were responsible for others' lives or for others' feelings. They developed an inaccurate perception that they could and should control others, and spent much of their time and energy trying to do just that. In her relationships with the sex addict, this woman often spent hours deciding which behavior on her part would produce the desired behavior in the addict. A woman might hide pornography, be sexual, or refuse to be sexual, insist that he attend church, make plans so he would have to come home, not make plans because she knew he wouldn't come home, or try other strategies, all designed to get the addict to live according to her design. Most of the time this maneuvering produced little, if any, positive result. Unfortunately, if it produced any positive result at all, the woman was reinforced in her belief that she could control the sex addict's life if she just tried hard enough.

"Live and Let Live" reminds you that you have no right and no power to control the addict's life. In trying to control, you are inevitably frustrated, and feel terrible about yourself. "Live and Let Live" gives you permission to let go of that control. As a result, the sex addict is forced to be responsible for his own life. As long as you suffer the consequences of his behavior by trying to control his life, he will not be motivated to change. Why should he?

An added benefit of allowing him to live his own life is that you no longer feel responsible for the disasters he brings on himself. It is only through his experiencing these disasters that he will reach out for help. One woman at a meeting described it this way: "I pictured the addict confronted with all kinds of problems, on the other side of which were happiness and wholeness. Then I pictured myself as though laying on the ground in front of him, blocking his path through his problems and keeping him from finding his way to happiness. I realized how unfair that was, both to him and to me, and I was able to stop doing it."

Easy Does It

"Easy Does It" is a useful tool for those women who love sex addicts who feel they must always try harder. Sometimes a woman needs to apply this slogan to old behavior. She may try harder to control the addict, yell a little louder at her children in an attempt to get them in line, or pile a little more on herself to keep things looking good on the surface. At other times, this slogan applies to actually working her recovery program. She may want to read everything now, and make all the necessary changes today. She wants to be different immediately, and she is harsh with herself when she isn't perfectly successful.

At such times, the woman who loves sex addicts can apply "Easy Does It." Most of these women spent 20, 30, or more years practicing the old behaviors; it is unrealistic to expect immediate change. Many changes in recovery come only over time. It's okay, as long as you're still working on recovery, to not have it all done. It never will be completed anyway, and insisting that you be further along than you are only causes you to feel bad about yourself a little more. Most women who love sex addicts don't need any more of that.

You can ease up on your emotions, too. It frequently seems that there are two extremes for women who love sex addicts. One will put tremendous energy into stuffing her feelings. When she applies "Easy Does It," she can stop trying so hard not to feel, and allow some emotions to surface. The other type of co-sex addict has no trouble expressing strong feelings, particularly anger, and may have used her feelings to manipulate and control those around her. She can apply "Easy Does It" as she realizes that getting all steamed up about things rarely produces the desired results anyway.

"Easy Does It," like so many of the program tools, helps create an atmosphere that encourages kindness toward yourself and others. When you apply "Easy Does It," you stop trying to force solutions in your own life and the lives of others, and begin to see that your higher power often provides solutions you never dreamed of. Daily application of "Easy Does It" can tremendously reduce the amount of stress in your life. Instead of creating or adding to crisis, you can allow solutions to happen.

Let Go and Let God

Women who love sex addicts spend a lot of time and energy trying to control the uncontrollable. They feel compelled to bring about change in the sex addict. They feel responsible for controlling or curing his addiction. They feel there should be something they can do to stop the problem that is causing them so much pain. With addictions, though, the harder they try to control, the worse things seem to get.

What a relief it is to learn in Twelve Step recovery that letting go is not only okay, but essential to your growth. You feel like the weight of the world is on your shoulders. Your life seems to be falling apart. There are countless situations that appear to require immediate answers. Not only do you not have all the answers, but new problems crop up, almost on a daily basis. Life feels crazy, you feel crazy, you feel totally overwhelmed.

"Let Go and Let God" may be a new concept to you. Some women who love sex addicts have felt abandoned by God. Some never had a consistent concept of a Higher Power at all. One woman said, "God certainly didn't care what was going on in my life, or He would have fixed my husband." This belief led her to continue trying to control her husband's acting out, and no matter what she did, it wasn't enough. She didn't have any faith that life would be better if she gave the situation to God, yet she desperately needed relief from the pain of living with an active sex addict. It was a painful place to be.

Letting go can feel like giving up. It can feel like you are condoning the behavior of the addict. In truth, "Let Go and Let God" simply means that you are acknowledging that you just don't have all the answers. You have been expecting yourself to treat a problem that many professionals don't even recognize or know how to treat. It is an unbearable burden to carry alone. By allowing yourself to let go, you lighten your load, and give God a chance to provide solutions to your problems.

Letting go is scary at first. You don't have any guarantees that things will turn out the way you think you want them to. And often in the beginning, when you do let go, situations can appear to get worse. When you are tempted to grab hold of the situation again, you can remind yourself that all your previous efforts to control did not bring about any significant positive changes. As you let go, one moment or one situation at a time, your faith in your Higher Power will grow, and it will be easier to let go in the future.

First Things First

Living with addiction creates chaos in the lives of women who love sex addicts. As they run from one crisis to another, they lose track of priorities. They are easily confused and overwhelmed. They start one project, but get distracted by another, or even by their own obsessive thoughts. They are so busy trying to put order into the addict's life that they neglect their own.

"First Things First" reminds a woman that there is a way out of the chaos created by the addict and her responses to him. It causes her to stop and consider where she is, and what steps she might need to take to get where she would like to be.

"First Things First" is a good tool to use when you first begin to feel overwhelmed. It's use can prevent further chaos from developing.

This slogan also reminds you that, all too often, you place yourself and your recovery last. You are very used to taking care of everyone around you. You may not, however, have a lot of experience at considering your own needs. "First Things First" allows you to place a high priority on your own health and well-being, without which you could never have a really satisfying relationship with the sex addict, or anybody else for that matter. It reminds you that your primary responsibility is to yourself, and allows you to place the responsibility for the addict's life where it belongs: with him.

Keep It Simple

"Keep It Simple" is a tool for those women who love sex addicts who complicate their lives by taking on too much at one time, or by worrying too much, or by making mountains out of molehills. Sound familiar? Co-sex addicts frequently do all of the above, in an attempt to fix what's wrong in their lives. Even a recovery program can be unnecessarily complicated. "Keep It Simple" is a reminder that often, the less you do about a situation, the better it turns out.

"Keep It Simple" slows you down, relieving much of the stress you pile on yourself. It streamlines your thought processes, which so often border on the obsessive. It reminds you, one more time, that you don't have to have all the answers to life's problems. It stops those "what if" tapes, and gives you back the energy you would otherwise waste complicating your life. It allows you to see reality a little more clearly.

The Serenity Prayer

"GOD, GRANT ME THE SERENITY TO ACCEPT THE THINGS I CANNOT CHANGE, THE COURAGE TO CHANGE THE THINGS I CAN, AND THE WISDOM TO KNOW THE DIFFERENCE."

So reads the prayer that many fellowships use to start or end their meetings. It is a recovery standard, and the topic of many, many meetings.

In recovery, a women who love sex addicts comes to realize that the only person she can change is herself. The Serenity Prayers reminds her that she has no power or authority over the sex addict or anyone else. She cannot change the fact that her partner is a sex addict. She cannot keep him from acting out. She cannot force him into recovery.

In addition, she can't change her history. If she was sexually abused as a child, she can't go back and change that. She can't make her parents into safe people if they weren't or aren't. So many women who love sex addicts keep trying. They adjust their behavior in order to get a certain response from others. Most of the time, other people are not capable of the response the woman is looking for anyway. Often, she is expecting healthy behavior from unhealthy people.

So if you can't change someone else's behavior, what can you change? You can change your thinking, your attitudes, and your future possibilities by applying the principles of Twelve Step recovery to your life. In short, you can change yourself. You can develop and nurture a relationship with a God of your understanding. You can find out what you're doing that's not working, and try new behaviors. You can support other women in recovery, helping them to change, and keeping yourself on track.

The Serenity Prayer reminds you to place your energies where they will be most effective. And it reminds you who to look to for the help you need: God.

For a long time in recovery you might have difficulty finding the wisdom to know the difference between what you can and cannot change. That is why you attend meetings and share with others what is going on in your life. God doesn't send you a memo with a list of what's yours to change and how you should go about doing it. God does, however, speak through other people, if you are willing to listen. In order to hear whatever message your Higher Power has for you, you need to place yourself where you can receive it. Meetings, therapy, and work with a sponsor are all good places to get the message.

Sponsorship

In Co-SA, as in other Twelve Step programs, members are encouraged to find a sponsor. A sponsor is a fellow member, whom you identify with, and who is working an active recovery program. It is frequently recommended that you find a sponsor who has already worked through the Twelve Steps.

A sponsor is part of your recovery "tool kit." She is someone you can talk to between meetings. She is an advisor as far as working your steps, and a frequent choice for hearing a fifth step. A good sponsor will be available to listen. She will suggest, but not advise. She will offer feedback, but not shame. She will be able to be real with the women she sponsors, and she will have a sponsor herself.

You may feel afraid to ask someone to sponsor you. You might feel as if you're not important enough for someone to spend time with. On the other hand, you might still be unwilling to really let someone know all that is going on with you. It is often said, "We are only as sick as the secrets we keep," and that is especially true where women who love sex addicts are concerned. You might not feel comfortable sharing your story with an entire group, but sharing with at least one person is important, and essential to your recovery.

It is not necessary to choose a sponsor right away. As you attend meetings, and listen to others share, you will probably hear someone you particularly admire or identify with. If you stay and talk with other members after the meetings, you will be able to see which members you are most comfortable with. If you are still unsure, ask someone to explain sponsorship to you, or ask that a meeting be about sponsorship.

It is all right to have more than one sponsor, and it is also all right to change sponsors. You don't have to feel compelled to pick just the right one. The important thing is to begin sharing yourself with someone. If you find you've chosen a sponsor you are uncomfortable with, you can change.

Many sponsor-sponsoree relationships become long-lasting friendships. For many women it is the first relationship they remember where they are valued and loved unconditionally. When you've been valued only if you were sexual, or only if you worked hard enough, it can be a real relief and a blessing to be valued just for being you.

24

The Twelve Steps

Now we enter into the recovery program known as the Twelve Steps. The original Twelve Steps were written over 50 years ago for Alcoholics Anonymous. These alcoholics, after some period of sobriety, decided to write down the principles and the steps they took to maintain their sobriety and to live a better, healthier life. These principles and steps have been used throughout the world to help millions and millions of people with various addictions such as narcotic abuse, overeating, emotional problems, co-dependency, and sexual addiction. We now refer to them for the woman who loves sex addicts as Co-sexual addiction recovery.

The Twelve Steps of Co-SA

(Reprinted with permission of Co-SA, Minneapolis, Minnesota)

1. We admitted we were powerless over our co-dependency with the sex addict, and that our lives had become unmanageable.
2. Came to believe that a power greater than ourselves could restore us to sanity.
3. Made a decision to turn our will and our lives over to the care of God, as we understood God.

4. Made a searching and fearless moral inventory of ourselves.
5. Admitted to God, to ourselves, and to another human being the exact nature of our wrongs.
6. Were entirely ready to have God remove all these defects of character.
7. Humbly asked God to remove our shortcomings.
8. Made a list of all persons we had harmed and became willing to make amends to them all.
9. Made direct amends to such people wherever possible, except when to do so would injure them or others.
10. Continued to take personal inventory, and when we were wrong, promptly admitted it.
11. Sought through prayer and meditation to improve our conscious contact with God as we understood God, praying only for knowledge of God's will for us and the power to carry that out.
12. Having had a spiritual awakening as the result of these steps, we tried to carry this message to others, and to practice these principles in all our day to day living.

An Interpretation of the Twelve Steps for Woman Who Love Sex Addicts

What we will attempt to do in the following pages is to express the principles and concepts of the Twelve Steps as they are used for recovery from sexual co-dependency, so that you can implement them in your personal recovery. Our comments here should not be construed as representing any particular Twelve Step fellowship. They are our own interpretation of the Steps. We will follow this with a personal Twelve Step recovery story from one co-sex addict.

Step One

We admitted we were powerless over our co-dependency with the sex addict, and that our lives had become unmanageable.

We admitted we were powerless. The steps are written in the past tense for a reason. Your mind hears the words, and begins to believe them before you are consciously aware of it. Saying "I've admitted something," is different than saying, "I can admit something." You mind hears it as being already done, and your thinking begins to change. What are you admitting in Step One? You are admitting powerlessness. People in recovery often say that lack of power is their dilemma. This is very true for co-sex addicts. There are many, many things the co-sex addict has tried to change unsuccessfully. They were unsuccessful because these were not their things to change. They used what power they did have inappropriately; they used it to try to change other people and circumstances. That is what you are powerless over: other people, places and things.

Our co-dependency. First note that this says *"our"*. This is an indication that you are not alone. You have felt lonely, and felt abandoned by people who you wish would care about you—including yourself—but you are not alone.

Co-dependency. There is that word again. You will see this word throughout the recovery process. What does it mean? One author has said that co-dependency is someone depending on someone else, someone who depends on something that is undependable. Others have said it is a need to be in a relationship in order to have a sense of identity or worth. Still others have said it is the need to control others or the environment, because of the amount of chaos in your internal being. Co-dependency can include some or all of these.

As a woman who loves sex addicts, you are admitting that you are dependent; that you have issues of control; that you get in and stay in relationships that are unhealthy for you—especially relationships with sex addicts. You come to a place where you admit that this is true. You cannot *not* get into relationships like this without help. You cannot *not* try to control without help. You cannot *not* give in to the demands of the sex addict without help. You must look at this with honesty and integrity, so you can move on to interdependence, and have healthier relationships.

With the sex addict. One of the better definitions of a sex addict is someone who depends on sex to meet his emotional needs, which he is unable to meet through healthy coping skills. A sex addict is someone you, as a co-sex addict, find yourself in relationships with. You find men who, no matter how often they have sex, are unable to get their needs met because the need is too great. It's a need in their heart, a need in their most inner self, that can't be fulfilled through sexual activity. If someone is connecting all the time in a sexual manner, if he has been sexually abused or exposed to pornography or other sexual behavior at an early age; if he has learned to use sex as a coping mechanism for stress and shame, and a way of connecting to another being without risking emotional vulnerability, he is a sex addict.

Women who love sex addicts can probably define a sex addict with no problem. Figuring out that the man you're involved with is a sex addict is a different issue. You will continue to need help in clarifying this issue as you enter new relationships, because time and time again, you will be attracted to the same type of man. This is part of your powerlessness.

And that our lives. Here in Step One it doesn't say my life or your life, it says *our* lives. Here again is the connection that you will feel as you sit in groups and hear others' stories. You are not alone. This pre-disposition to find yourself in relationships with sex addicts is a common bond between yourself and other women who love sex addicts. It is something that all of you share. You have all come together to get help for the same issue. Having this common issue strengthens you and gives you hope. You are not alone in recovery, and you are not alone in being a woman who loves a sex addict. Many women love sex addicts. Our culture is permeated with them, so it is a common phenomenon to love a sex addict.

Had become. "Become" indicates a process. Co-dependency with sex addicts is not something that just happened one day. It is not something that necessarily happened in just one relationship, although it could have. In most cases it is something that involved time, low self-esteem, a lack of nurturing, abuse or traumatization, and not believing you're worthy of being in a healthy relationship. All of these characteristics take time to develop. If you are now in a period of your life when it has become unmanageable, you should remember that you have engaged in a process that evolved, eventually, into unmanageability. As it has taken time to get where you are, it is going to take time to get well. As one sponsor said to her sponsoree, "You didn't get here in a day, and you're not going to get well in a day." You're going to begin to see a process of growth as you recognize your powerlessness and how you became the way you are.

Unmanageable. Unmanageability is sometimes hard for a woman who loves sex addicts to see. Often she has created a pristine environment, either at home and dependent, or out in the world and independent, in control, and apparently confident. A woman may have her social friends, maybe some darling children, possibly even some positive relationships, but everything is set up so that it looks good.

How can something that looks so good on the surface be unmanageable? The secret is that the unmanageability is on the inside, where a woman may feel confusion, anger, bitterness, frustration and uncertainty. She can't leave her sex addict because she doesn't know if she'll get her emotional needs met, or where she'll get her financial needs met. Inside, she is scared, often lonely, and usually isolated from real relationships. This is inner unmanageability.

In addition, she is not able to define and maintain boundaries in her relationship. She doesn't know where she ends and he begins, where her needs end and his take over. She can't say no when she doesn't want to have sex. This is outer unmanageability.

Women who love sex addicts frequently find themselves in unfulfilling, sexualized relationships. They engage in physical sexual acts but don't experience any real intimacy. It's hard for a woman who loves sex addicts to look at this kind of life and realize how many years she may have operated in these patterns of making poor choices. In realizing her unmanageability, though, she comes to want recovery and to ask for help. She finally realizes that she can't do it by herself. Many of these women recognize that the messes they have made are so large that they need help to clean them up.

In this sense, unmanageability is positive. It is the dirt road that leads you to the highway of recovery. It is always good, if you live in the woods, to have a dirt road to lead you to the highway. It is a positive thing to be on the road to recovery as you begin to understand your unmanageability. For some women, making a list of how their lives are unmanageable is helpful. It keeps them from making the same mistakes again, and slipping back into denial.

Step Two

Came to believe that a power greater than ourselves could restore us to sanity.

Came to believe. Again, notice the step is written in the past tense. The original steps were written to share the process that the original members of AA went through in recovery. There was a process through which they came to believe.

It is really a simple process. You come to believe many things in your life. For example, you came to believe that there was a Santa Claus; later you came to believe that there wasn't a Santa Claus. As you grew older, you may have come to believe that a certain boy liked you, and later realized he didn't like you. We come to believe certain religious and political positions. There is some consistency to this process throughout our lives. In this process, there is a definite point at which you understand or come to believe.

In Twelve Step groups, the process of coming to believe is something that often happens as a result of exposure to other recovering people. You may not necessarily know the date or the hour when you did come to believe, but you know that you feel differently, and you begin to have hope. This is so important in recovery, because knowing that you have come to believe, or knowing you do believe, can save your life. Women who love sex addicts can get down, feel hopeless or worthless, experience severe shame and guilt from past traumas or present circumstances, and resort to sad behaviors of destruction, isolation, sexual acting out, and suicidal ideation. If you have come to believe, you have hope that something out there cares for you, loves and accepts you.

A power. "A" is a common word. You use it every day. A cat, a dog, a book—and in every context in which it is used, it denotes *one*. If you were going to use a word to describe more than one, you would say "the," "these," or another word that indicates plurality. This step is not written in the plural. It says *a* Higher Power. This is significant. Seeing *a* here, you realize that there is one entity, one strength, one energy, on spirit, one power. It is significant that as you come to believe, you are believing in one. It is important to note that each individual must come to believe in the *one* that feels right to her.

Greater than ourselves. This is one of the first areas which requires trust from the woman who loves sex addicts. She now knows that there is one that is greater than herself. This is the best news she has had in recovery: that she doesn't have to figure this out alone. As you begin to trust this power, you begin to recover from the sick patterns, poor choices and undesirable relationships that have been so much a part of your past.

In the original context, this power greater than ourselves indicated that the power was greater than that first group of recovering alcoholics. This one single power was greater than a whole group. That's a lot of power. Women in recovery frequently first recognize this power in the group, but it is greater than the group. Even if you had a Higher Power before, you may have had difficulty accessing the resources of that Higher Power and applying it to your life. In the program, you come to believe that this Higher Power has more ability to solve life's problems than you do individually. What a relief!

Could. "Could" is one of the most hopeful, loving expressions in the Twelve Steps. Could this Higher Power have the ability, the resources, the energy, the intention of helping you along in the recovery process? It is possible now to begin to be restored; it is possible now to begin to be healthy, and to have loving relationships with loving people, to be loved and nurtured in a healthy way. It can be done, and the Higher Power can do it. It is the experience of many, many women in recovery that, if given the freedom and the opportunity—in other words if you quit trying to do it all on your own—this Higher Power *will* do for you what you have been unable or unwilling to do for yourself. All you have to do is ask.

Restore us to sanity. "Restore" means bringing something back. Frequently when you think of restoration, you think of restoring an automobile or an old house, and making it look like new. The same is true of recovery.

Women who love sex addicts have for so long been robbed of spirituality, intimacy, trust, and even their own reality. In a world that should have been safe, they were violated again and again. And then they were told they hadn't been violated. They began to feel crazy. Recovery brings them right to where they need to be: restored to sanity.

Insanity is natural when you live with a disease as crazy as sexual addiction. You may have difficulty applying the idea of insanity to yourself, when the addict is the one who looks crazy. But trying to have a sane response to an insane situation makes you begin to feel crazy. You try again and again to do something that should work, but doesn't. You try and try to fix the problems the sex addict creates in your life. You confront, complain, threaten, abandon, refuse to abandon, feel guilty, cry, laugh, rage. It seems like that would be enough to change his behavior. In a situation that doesn't involve a disease, these behaviors might work. But sexual addiction is a disease. None of these behaviors can change a disease.

The behaviors themselves are not insane, but the fact that you use them again and again, never stopping to realize that they're not working, qualifies you to be restored to sanity. It is possible for women who love sex addicts to be restored to sanity. Those already in recovery have experienced it. They are living proof that it is possible to make better choices, and we hope, as you read this, you know that it is possible for you. You may still feel crazy, but if you have gotten this far in this book, you have a good chance at finding sanity, even in an insane relationship.

Step Three

> **Made a decision to turn our wills and our lives over to the care of God, as we understood God.**

Made. "Made" is kind of like "become"; it indicates a process which involves time and choices, but there is definitely a time when it is done. For example, when kids in school make an ashtray, or a meal in cooking class, or a dress, there is a time when it is in the process of being made, and then it is completed. It is made. "Made" is something that has been coming along, but is finally resolved to the point that you can say it's done.

A. Here again we come to that little word, *"a"*. It is one. What we are discussing in Step Three is a one time event. Many people want to spread this step out, but as you move along in this process of working the steps, you will see why we only make this decision one time.

Decision. When you make a decision you list the good and the bad, the pros and cons of a situation. In this step, you can make a list of what you have done with your life in the past, and how you could deal with your life differently in the future. Such a list makes it easier to make the decision you are asked to make in Step Three. It is *a* decision.

Compare it to a traditional courtship and marriage. It's like you had an engagement period in Step Two, during which you get to know your Higher Power, and began to get comfortable with the idea of having God in your life. Step Three is the marriage ceremony itself, where you make a commitment to share your life with God. You just have a single ceremony, but it sets the stage for further development through the relationship. Step Three asks you to be willing to share your life with God. The decision is a one time event, but it provides a means for further growth.

To turn. Turning can be expressed in many ways. Someone said once that turning means, "to flip over," kind of like a hotcake. The hotcake gets done on one side, and then you have to turn it over.

It is a pretty simple definition of turn, but it is also pretty profound. It you flip over, you make a total change from the way you have been up to this point. "Turn" is used on highways all over the world to indicate direction: signs indicate left or right turn, or U- turn. When you make a U-turn, you turn around and go in the opposite direction. What you do in Step Three is definitely a U-turn! It is a turning in the opposite direction. You turn away from all your limited understanding of how life should be. You leave behind perceptions, experiences, and ideas about things you thought you understood. You turn from them and gain a whole new perspective. This is an essential part of recovery. You are turning into something, or turning somewhere else, and it is amazing how far that turn can take you, as you continue in your recovery efforts.

Our will. Again there is a plural here, as the group stays and works together. In this group of safe people who have turned their wills and lives over to God you will begin to see this decision as a possibility for yourself. But what is your will? "Will's" simplest definition is probably your choices—the choices that you make for your life. In the group you begin to turn over the choices that you make to God. This can be an easy thing for some, but for others it can be a very hard thing to do. It means you must turn your choices over to God, try to understand God's perspective, and follow that perspective in your life. That is why Step Three is so powerful.

In many recovery groups there is a phrase called "stinking thinking." Stinking thinking is the way an addict, alcoholic or a non-recovering person thinks. This thinking doesn't work. The choices non-recovering people make don't bring about positive results; there seems to be a certain self-destructiveness to their choices and behavior. Step Three cuts the cord of stinking thinking. It is the beginning of a new lifestyle.

Giving up your own will is a way of having a safety valve for co-sex addicts. In making decisions about relationships and making decisions about dependency, the co-sex addict is now able to turn to God. As she does, God will demonstrate new directions she can take, and new choices she can make. She will begin getting answers, and will be able to make different choices about her behavior around sex addicts. This is a freedom that is only gained by letting go of your own will, or choices.

Our lives. Our lives are the result of all our choices. For each individual woman, life is the totality of all parts of herself. When you turn it all over—spiritually, emotionally, physically, in relationships, socially, and financially—you give yourself to God. You begin to trust God. You begin to believe that God will take care of you.

You may say this is frightening: "How can I trust God?" But simply look at what you have trusted in the past. You have trusted your own ability to think, your own ability to make choices. You have taken the advice of a few chosen people who have not necessarily acted in your best interests. You may have depended totally on the sex addict, getting from him your self-esteem and your value. You turned your choices over to the sex addict and allowed him to decide whether you could go to school, what you would do during the day, and whether you could have this or that.

Many co-sex addicts have turned their lives over to other things. Some have turned their lives over to perfectionism, control, and addictive substances like alcohol, drugs, sex, overeating, or gambling. They have turned their lives over to these people, substances, or behaviors with relative ease, with no fuss, and with very little fear. But when faced with a positive relationship with one who does have the ability to restore them to sanity, they go with trepidation. They go with the garbage of the past trailing behind them, trying to pull them back.

Turning your will and life over is necessary. It is through this trust experience with God that you begin to believe that God loves you. You begin once again to trust yourself. Eventually, you can even regain your trust in men. Step Three is an essential part of working the steps. It is not a luxury. It is necessary for a healthy, happy life. Working the steps is not always easy, and often you do not understand why you must work them. Often the steps are understood only after they have been completed. Then you realize the beauty of this spiritual process, and open yourself to further growth and joy as you walk this road with others making the same steps toward recovery.

The care of God. What do you think of when you hear the word "care?" It's often expressed in terms of someone who loves you; someone who demonstrates some kindness toward you; someone who is willing to get involved in your life, willing to get in there and be patient with you; to work with you and not condemn you in the process; someone who can be nurturing. All these pictures of a loving parent or a loving friend can represent care. Care is felt in the release of energy from one person to another, usually through kind behaviors, like providing a listening ear or some other sign of concern.

How does this relate to God? What is the care of God? It is simply God's willingness to be involved in a nurturing, supportive, accepting way in your life. God is concerned for the woman who loves sex addicts. God's concern for others in this world demonstrates that care. You can sometimes see it more clearly in the lives of others than you can in your own life. For some women who love sex addicts, the group is a manifestation of the care of God in their lives. It is possible for you to connect with this issue that so radically changes your life by looking at others in your support group. Something as simple as their support can be seen as the extension of God's care and concern.

Now, we get to *God*. The original writers of the Twelve Steps changed only one word from their initial version. That word was in Step Two. They changed the word "God" to "a Power greater than ourselves." That is the only change they made, and it was made for this reason: those first alcoholics said that God was too scary for the recovering person in Step Two. Maybe the recovering person had had too many hurts, too many problems with God, so the word was changed to, "a Power greater than ourselves," to give the newcomer an engagement period, and allow her to experience God through the group's care, nurturing and love. In this way she could come to believe in a caring God who could, and would, help her.

But who is God? Each woman will define this for herself. Let us share our thoughts with you on this subject. Simply put, God is Love. God is also in authority or in control, especially for those who turn their lives and will over, and switch the authority from themselves to God.

According to what you have learned so far in the steps, God has the ability to restore you. God is more powerful than you are alone, or in a group. God is one who gets actively involved in your life, who has more power and more success than you in dealing with sex addicts. This God can and will help you as you work the Twelve Steps.

For many, this understanding of God will develop into a faith that is common to our culture, and will enable the recovering co-sex addict to enjoy the benefits of finding a community that shares her same faith. Some will not. It is a universal blessing of this program, however, that they will, if they are willing, come to a greater relationship with God as they understand God.

The people who have turned their wills and lives over to the care of a God they understand—who have turned their choices over to God—often have more understanding of how

God works and how God thinks. The group is a good resource, especially for those early in recovery who want an understanding of God. It is very important to realize, as it pertains to understanding God, that no single person is going to understand the totality of God, but the members of your support group can be seen as different reflections of God.

As we understood God. One way to interpret this is to compare your understanding of God with the way you function in relationships with people, because we are talking about a relationship. When you first meet someone, your knowledge of them is limited. Only through time, communication, and commitment to any relationship do you really come to understand another person. The same is true in your relationship with God. Coming to understand God is a process which is available to any and all in recovery who are willing to turn their will and life over, so that they can experience a new life, a new freedom, and find happiness. The beauty of finding God in the Twelve Steps is that as you grow, your understanding of God grows too.

Step Four

Made a searching and fearless moral inventory of ourselves.

Made a searching. Searching holds the possibility of fun, but for women who love sex addicts, searching can be extremely painful. When you search, you intend to find something. For example, when you lose your keys, you go searching, with the intent of finding the keys. As you begin your inventory, you are searching, you are scrutinizing, you are seeking with intent to find something that is significant.

In this context, "searching" indicates that you will have to expend some energy. This is the beginning of what is often referred to in the program as the "action steps." You now begin to take action in your own behalf. Note that this step is also in the past tense. As you begin your inventory, you can know that others have passed this way before, and have survived and gotten better. You are not alone.

Fearless. In the word "fearless," the suffix "less" means "without." For example, "jobless" is without a job. "Fearless" simply means without fear. This is the attitude with which you approach your moral inventory. Being fearless allows you to view your inventory objectively, as you uncover the pain. You will be looking at what was done to you, and what you have done to yourself and others.

Many of the experiences you will be looking at are extremely painful. For some, the painful experience was childhood sexual abuse; for others it was forced oral sex or rape. For some, it will be something they would much rather not ever remember, something they may think they only imagined. Fearlessness will lead you to look at your own part in the sick relationships you have been in as an adult, and at the patterns that have repeated over and over in your life. You need to look at these things with an attitude of courage and bravery. You can, because in Step Three you turned your will and life over to the care of a loving God.

Moral. "Moral" can be defined as right and wrong, categories of black and white, or good and bad. Something that is immoral could be defined as something that violates your conscience. As you look at your life in Step Four, you will be looking for things that you've done that have violated your conscience. For example, as kids many of us had the experience of raiding the cookie jar. We knew that we were not supposed to get a cookie. There might not be anything wrong with having a cookie, but we were told not to, so it became wrong. Yet we waited until our parents could not see, and took a cookie anyway. It probably tasted good, but we may have felt bad afterwards. We felt bad because we knew we did something wrong.

This is a simple example, but many women who love sex addicts have had similar experiences with their sexuality. Your partner may have told you that the sexual acts he was suggesting were okay, but at some internal place these acts violated the standards that you had set for yourself, or which were set for you by your parents. You participated, maybe even willingly, but afterwards, you felt guilt, remorse, and shame. You no longer felt good about yourself.

In Step Four you will also be looking at how you were violated by others. Have you ever said to yourself, "If they really knew me, they wouldn't like me. If they knew I was sexually abused or raped, they wouldn't be my friend." The shame and guilt you carry from the actions of other people toward you can be overwhelming. Step Four is designed to release you from that shame and guilt as you look at how your moral code has been violated by others through sexual abuse or rape.

It is wrong to believe that you are unworthy because of your past. In recovery, you come to know yourself and let others know you. Step Four is about coming to know yourself, being honest with yourself about what happened, taking into account how it affected your life, and where it leaves you today. In short, Step Four is an inventory. You will list everything that happened, even if it involved others and you were just an innocent bystander—as in the case of divorce of your parents, or the death of a grandparent or other significant family member. Such an event may not have had anything to do with *your* morals, but it did affect you emotionally.

Inventory. What are you to inventory in Step Four? You inventory your experiences because, as a human being, that is what you have on hand. You inventory your memory, for that is what you have been given to record your experiences. Many see this inventory as a life story. It is a process where you begin to see the truth of what you've done, and what has been done to you. Some things will be negative, others will be positive. When a storekeeper takes inventory, he lists not only the things he wants to get rid of, but the things he wants to keep. And he doesn't just make a mental note of it—he *writes it down.*

Step Four is a written assignment. You will need to have pen or pencil, paper, and a quiet place where you can be uninterrupted. Some women just begin writing. Some organize their inventory by ages, such as zero to six years, six to twelve years, and so on. Still others have done it by first listing all the traumatic events they can remember—things that were done to them or by them that violated their value system—and then writing how they felt at the time, and how they feel now about those events. There is no right or wrong way to write an inventory. The important thing is just to do it. You will be face to face for perhaps the first time with the total reality of your life. It can be pretty overwhelming, so don't be afraid to let your sponsor or therapist know how you are feeling while writing. As you transfer your story to paper, you are also transferring the pain, guilt and shame to paper too. Writing an inventory can be a very positive experience, and it is vital to your continued recovery.

Of ourselves. Once again, you see the plural, and know that others have done this before. You can survive the pain of writing your inventory down. It is so joyous to see others freed from their shame. As you see other members of your support groups complete their inventories, you will begin to believe that this release from shame can happen for you, too. You are reminded that only you can do this for yourself. Only you know your pain, the strength of your fears, your deepest secrets. Only you are qualified to write this inventory. Many women have had their inventory taken by the sex addict for years. Now is your time to decide for yourself who you are, and who you want to be. There is great freedom in taking your focus off of what's wrong with the sex addict, and doing a searching and fearless moral inventory of yourself. You may not understand the value of this step until you have completed it, but it is well worth the pain and tears.

Step Five

Admitted to God, to ourselves, and to another human being the exact nature of our wrongs.

Admitted. Here you are again, looking at that word, "admitted." You already know that it means to, "fess up," or acknowledge what is already true. You may have already experienced the pain and joy of doing this, probably as a child or adolescent. Perhaps you put yourself in a situation you knew your parents would not approve of, or did something wrong, and knew you were going to have to tell them, because you knew they were going to find out anyway. Do you remember your feelings of guilt and shame, like you had let yourself and them down? Then you somehow got the courage to tell them what you had done. You admitted the truth—no matter the consequences. It felt better, finally, to let the secret out.

The same is true in Step Five. You admit all that you have written in your Fourth step. You let out all those secrets and finally feel that clean joy which comes from truly being totally known.

To God. God might be the easiest person to tell, or the hardest, depending on your relationship with God. If you feel God has let you down before, admitting what's been wrong in your life can be particularly difficult. Fortunately, God has a reputation for being forgiving of all that you have done, and being willing to restore any lost part of yourself back to him. As one wise person in recovery stated, "It's okay to tell God. God already knows it all anyway, and is just waiting for us to be honest about it, too."

To ourselves. Admitting your past secrets to yourself often takes place as you write your Fourth step, if you are truly fearless and thorough when writing it. Admitting your powerlessness, your need to be restored to sanity, your profound amazement at your poor choices, and your sincere sense of having failed yourself is probably the most humbling experience you will have with regard to your sense of who you are.

It is at this point, though, that the recovery of your true self is able to take an upward turn, without the overwhelming sense of shame or guilt that has been so closely bound to you in the past. You are now able to begin a more shame-free life, which empowers you to experience the next and most essential part of this step: being able to reveal yourself to another human being.

And to another human being. *"What?* I have to tell all this stuff to somebody else, face to face?" you're asking. Telling your story to another human being is the most crucial part of your recovery. In writing your Fourth Step, you have taken your total history of shame, hurt, abandonment, abuse and poor choices, and poured it consciously into one place. Your Fourth Step may even have brought to your conscious awareness some things you have been suppressing for years, and now all of these memories are in one place. If all this pain is kept inside the woman who loves a sex addict, and is not shared with another human being, she may talk herself into believing once again that she is unlovable or unacceptable with such a painful, messy past. She could use this information and history for condemnation instead of healing. That is why she must tell another person. She must realize that she is loved and accepted even though she has been places and experienced things she is not proud of.

In this Fifth Step you experience spiritually, emotionally, and often physically, a cleansing or a lightening of your load. As you share who you have been and what you have experienced with another trusted person, you are reassured that there is nothing you have done which makes you unlovable. Now someone knows the whole truth, and still loves you. It is remarkable!

A note of caution is appropriate here: when you choose someone to hear your Fifth Step, it is important to pick the least condemning, most loving and accepting person you know. You might choose a therapist, sponsor, or spiritual person you trust. Choose someone who understands that you are digging into your past in order to make your present and future better—someone who will not shame you for your past.

The exact nature of our wrongs. The fact that this part of the step is so specific will help two kinds of people: those who say, "I can't be specific so I'll never really feel loved," and those who believe that they can own everybody else's wrongs and avoid looking at their own choices. The first person needs to be specific in sharing her story, because the shame she experiences around the past is tied to specific episodes. She must talk about those specific episodes to relieve the shame associated with them. The second woman needs to acknowledge her own shortcomings and "clean her own side of the street"—not anyone else's—so that she too can be freed from her own shame. It's a recognized fact that you can't free anyone else from their shame. Each woman has to work her own program of recovery in order to have the kind of happy and fulfilling life they are all capable of experiencing.

Step Six

Were entirely ready to have God remove all these defects of character.

Were entirely ready. As you move from Step One through Step Five you discover a process through which you recognize powerlessness, find a Higher Power, a God of your understanding, go inside yourself by writing an inventory, and let someone else know who you really are. The very core of the program is in the first five steps. By working these steps you have learned to, "trust God and clean house."

Now that you have cleaned house, you must learn how to maintain your new surroundings. It is one process to clean a dirty house, whether you got it dirty yourself or just inherited all the mess—and it is another thing entirely to make sure it never gets that dirty again. That is what Step Six and the following steps are about: preventative maintenance.

You start by "being entirely ready." This simply means that you are 100% ready to look at the damage that was done by all that trash, and you evaluate what you can throw away. You might be quite attached to some of that stuff. Even though it doesn't work any longer, you hesitate to give it up. Someday, some of those old behaviors might come in handy, you keep thinking. You forget that each time you try old behavior it causes great pain. "Were entirely ready" indicates that you are finally tired of the pain. You finally realize that changing is not quite as frightening as staying the same.

To have God. Having God in their lives is so significant for women who love sex addicts. Here in Step Six they are reminded that they, like everyone, are blessed by having a relationship with God. They are beginning to believe that God does want the best for them, and that God wants their lives to express this new way of feeling and believing about themselves. God is willing to work with you, as you continue your efforts at recovery.

Remove all. This sounds like an unrealistic, maybe even painful statement, at least from a human standpoint. "Remove" indicates loss. Co-sex addicts have certainly experienced loss in their lives. But to lose, or remove, all of their defects? How?

Well, it isn't up to you to decide how, it's only up to you to be ready. Remember that earlier you recognized that you don't have a whole lot of power of your own. In Step Six you will rely on God to have the power to change you—the power you've been unable to access.

Defects of character. As you consider the term, "defects of character," you might be thinking of some of the ways you have behaved and felt that didn't work very well. Go ahead and get a pencil and paper and write down what comes to mind. Reviewing your inventory should give you a good idea of things about your character you might want changed.

For example, perhaps the way you express your anger indicates a defect of character. Maybe the way you control, and try to manipulate, your spouse or children; or the way you pout to get your own way; or isolate or run away from responsibility for yourself, are things you want to change. Honesty is important in listing these defects, because the ones you hold on to will keep you stuck in old patterns, and you will continue to attract unhealthy people into your life, especially in intimate relationships.

It is the experience of recovering co-sex addicts that as they become more healthy and honest themselves, they gravitate toward more healthy, honest people, and are better able to determine who is unhealthy. Understanding this can certainly motivate you to really look at your defects of character, and be 100% willing to have God remove them. This is the real release that prevents the dust and trash from resettling in your house.

Step Seven

Humbly asked God to remove our shortcomings.

Humbly. Many women struggle with the word, "humble," having been humiliated time and again by the sex addict. Humility is not the same as humiliation, although you may feel something like humiliation as you see the devastation caused by your defects of character, in your own life and the lives of those around you. Humility, in this case, means recognizing your true humanness. You see in Step Seven the manner with which you should approach God. Humility means knowing that you don't have the power to change yourself, but that God does. You come into God's presence with a humble heart, but with hope as well. And as you ask, you shall receive. As long as you don't have preconceived ideas of just how and when God will remove your defects of character, you will have them removed.

Asked God. Humility requires that we *ask*, not tell God anything. By now perhaps you have come to believe that God really does want the best for you; wants you to be free of your defects of character; wants you to feel good about yourself, and to be attracted to healthy people. You are asking, in a sense, to do God's will.

To remove our shortcomings. In Step Six you became ready. Now you push the "Go" button, and ask God to take your defects of character, or shortcomings. It would be nice if it happened all at once, but again you will experience it as a process. In this process God will be with you throughout your life, removing your shortcomings as you continue to identify them when they surface, as long as you are willing to ask for help.

For some women, this step comes easily. For others, it is very hard, especially if a woman is holding on, still rationalizing, still defending herself, still gripping her defense mechanisms. In that case, Step Seven can be a painful experience. As one woman said in a meeting, "There was never anything I let go of that didn't have claw marks all over it, including my defects of character."

You can trust that if you ask, God *will* remove your defects of character, no matter how much you resist. If you decide to hold on to them, you will be fighting a losing battle. It is at this point that you will really need your support group. They will give you valuable feedback about any shortcomings they see you holding on to. If you aren't sure, ask questions. Ask, "Am I still denying that my spouse is acting out? Am I trying to hold on to my Pollyanna life? Am I trying to control his behavior and shame him by being so innocent?" They will also give you support as you try new behaviors in place of the old ones that kept you so unhappy. Allow them to support you in this growth process.

Step Eight

Made a list of all persons we had harmed, and became willing to make amends to them all.

Made a list. You probably don't have any problem shopping for groceries if you've made a list. You know that the most efficient way to shop is to have a written list, instead of just a mental note, because otherwise you are likely to get home and find you have forgotten some essential items. There is a saying in Alcoholics Anonymous that you should be fearless and thorough from the very start. This is true in Step Eight. Again, you take pencil and paper in hand, and looking at your inventory, make a list of all those you have harmed. This list should include yourself as well as others, and can also include what damage was done, the person's name, and how they can be reached (telephone number, address, etc.). At this point, however, you only make the list.

Of all persons. Here again is that sometimes scary word: all. "All" means every single one. You are, once again, being challenged to be honest. To the degree that you can be honest in making this list, you will have hope for new relationships with important people in your life.

We had harmed. It takes an honest woman to look at her life and see the people she has harmed. It is often easier to see how you have been harmed by others. In Steps Four and Five you looked at how you have been hurt by trusted people in your life; how you have been traumatized; how you have been emotionally abandoned, and how you have suffered. But if all you look at is how you have been harmed, you are only halfway healed.

Just as it can be painful for a recovering alcoholic to see how his drinking damaged those around him, so it can be painful for the recovering co-sex addict to realize that what she has done has hurt others. For many women who love sex addicts, it is much more comfortable to be the victim. As a matter of fact, they have often been the victim of their own behavior, and of their own past, and even recent relationships. But past victimization by others just makes it that much more difficult for these women to realize that they have actually harmed other people. Perhaps they smothered them with concern, or more likely, control. Maybe through manipulation the women who love sex addicts didn't allow others to make healthy or growth producing decisions. Sometimes merely her silence about what was going on damaged others, most probably her children. The harm can be very subtle; you need to really search your mind and heart, in order to complete your healing.

And became willing. The past tense here reminds you, one more time, that the hard work demanded in the previous steps is

210

survivable. Women have worked their way through these steps before, and have found peace and happiness on the other side. It also indicates a process. Recovery doesn't just happen overnight. Becoming willing takes time for everyone, especially if they are holding on to a victim status.

To make amends. What does it mean to make amends? For women who love sex addicts, or anyone in recovery for that matter, to make amends means to acknowledge the wrong they have done, and be willing to be different. You stop blaming the other person to justify your own behavior. You stop rationalizing, and defending yourself. You stop avoiding responsibility. You are continuing to change in your relationships with yourself and others. You take full responsibility for what you have done, and to whom you have done it, at least on paper at this point.

To them all. Here is that word, "all" again. It seems to appear everywhere throughout the steps. By now your list should include everyone who has in any way been harmed by your actions or lack of action. You should have found the willingness to be different with each person on that list, including yourself. No stone should be left unturned at this point, or you will still carry old guilt that will keep you stuck in old sick patterns of thinking and relating. With names, phone numbers, and accounts of damages in hand, you are ready to move on.

Step Nine

Made direct amends to such people wherever possible, except when to do so would injure them or others.

Made direct amends. In Step Eight, you made your list. Now you go to the grocery store. In Step Nine, you actually go to the people on your list and make direct amends to them for the inappropriate attitudes or behaviors you have had in the past that have affected them. Notice again that this step is written in the past tense. These steps were written in the late 1930's when the first members of Alcoholics Anonymous became sober. Working these steps, especially Step Nine, was something they had to do to maintain their sobriety, so they would not have to carry the pain, shame or guilt of the past or present into their new sober lives.

They had to be honest with themselves. So do you, as you go to each person on your list and ask them for their forgiveness. When you acknowledge how your behavior affected your relationships with them, you will find the most incredible freedom. Tremendous emotional weights can be lifted, and often relationships can be restored, as the result of working Step Nine. This is not a 100% guarantee, since some relationships will remain fractured. However, at least your side of the street will be clean.

You will begin to feel wholeness and happiness in your life, now that you have made the effort to vent completely, without expectations. This is a significant point: you do not make amends with the expectation that your sex addict, friends, or family will change their behavior. You do not make amends with the expectation that people will respond in any certain way. People may, in fact, respond when you make amends, but it is by no means the motivation for you to do what you must to get rid of the stuff you've been carrying for so long.   Inflated expectations can cause you much pain, because others are not always in the same place with their recovery that you are with yours.   Many people do not choose a path of recovery at all. Your personal efforts and behavior however, can challenge them into this kind of recovery at some point.

It is not a given that the other person will ask forgiveness in return, even though they may have injured you much more than you have injured them.   Your goal is to clean your own slate. You are not responsible for what others leave undone, nor can their shortcomings keep you from recovering and feeling good about yourself.

Except when to do so would injure them or others. When you get to this point, you may become confused when you attempt to decide if making amends will injure the person involved, or be detrimental to other, possibly innocent, people. Such confusion is best resolved with the assistance of a group, sponsor, or therapist. Confusion is not to be used, however, as an excuse to not make any amends because you don't want to experience the pain or shame of admitting your past behavior.

What you must consider is whether or not your confession of earlier behavior would so significantly damage the other person that you should not bring the issue up. Go over your list with a sponsor, support group, or therapist. Ask, "Would this be damaging?" If you have a question, do not assume you have the answer. You could very possibly avoid an amend which could restore a relationship, or hold on to an amend that will set you up for old behavior.

Step Ten

Continued to take personal inventory and when we were wrong, promptly admitted it.

Continued. Here, again you must deal with the maintenance of your newly clean house. You are not letting the dust fall. You are not letting the dirt collect, or the garbage overflow in the can. Here you are in a process, as in Steps Four and Five. Today, when you have been inappropriate or have violated anyone's boundaries, including your own, you don't have to wait five or ten years to make amends. You can do it as you go along.

To take personal inventory. Taking a daily personal inventory is a process in which the woman who loves sex addicts is able to look at each person in her life, and see how she is interacting with this person. She looks at her attitudes toward others and honestly evaluates them. This is not done to the point where she is unable to enjoy interactions, but it is an honest evaluation of how she is responding to her peers, family, and in all her other relationships. It also is a reminder that you inventory only your own behavior, not that of others.

And when we were wrong, promptly admitted it. You will be wrong. This says, "when," not, "if," you were wrong. Many women who love sex addicts have been wronged, but there will still be times when you will be wrong yourself. It is so important for the recovering person to stay free, and not enter into a place of guilt and shame which can push her into some acting out behavior. So, in the maintenance of the Tenth Step, when you are wrong, you promptly admit it. "Promptly" is significant because it keeps you from holding on to the baggage, thinking for months about whether you were or weren't wrong. Promptly means admit it right now, right here. If you have been acting inappropriately, say, "I'm sorry. Forgive me, I'm acting inappropriately." It's as simple as that. Step Ten gives you a way to stay free from the bondage of guilt and shame. It keeps you humble, which often helps you to remain healthy.

Step Eleven

Sought through prayer and meditation to improve our conscious contact with God as we understood God, praying only for knowledge of God's will for us and the power to carry that out.

Sought through prayer and meditation. This step not only tells you what you are doing, but it tells you how to do it. You are seeking. You are looking to improve your relationship with God. The step tells you to do that through prayer and meditation. Prayer is that verbal, and sometimes internal, communication with God. It is such a positive experience for the woman who loves sex addicts to become more aware of God in her life. This step lets you know that it is your responsibility. Seeking requires action on your part. You may have felt abandoned by God, as you put no real effort into trying to find out where God was. It has been said many times in meetings, "If you can't find God, think who moved." You move away from God, God never moves away from you. Seeking is all that is required.

Meditation is a sometimes deeper sense of prayer. Prayer is requesting, asking, interacting. Meditation is listening, hearing God's voice. A lot of humans experience rest and peace through meditation, and are able to still the constant obsessive thinking that prevents them from hearing what God has to say: that they are significant, they are loved, they deserve to be healthy. Meditate on God's character, on your personal relationship with God, on some scripture or recovery material you have, allowing them to really sink in to your spirit. Be still, and God *will* speak to you.

To improve our conscious contact with God. Most women who love sex addicts, like many people, have an unconscious contact with God. They rely most of the time on their own thinking and resources, and connect with God only after they have thoroughly botched their lives. Step Eleven reminds you to keep God in your conscious mind. You are then able to experience the power and love of God in a whole new way; as a result, you experience life in a whole new way. You have a higher sense of purpose and joy. The result of this new awareness of God on a moment to moment basis is a better relationship with God. As with any relationship, efforts at improving the relationship require time, energy, and some sort of communication. With time you will find the method of communication that works best for you. There is no right or wrong way to do it. Just do it.

As we understood God. It is impossible for any one of us to totally understand God. Indeed, my understanding of God might not work for you, or yours for me. The beauty of the program is that you can begin to see evidence of God in other people. Remember this is not a job you undertake on your own. You come to a new understanding of God as you interact with the people in your support group, church, or other community of people seeking knowledge of God. As you listen, you will grow in understanding through other people's experiences of God in their lives.

Praying only for knowledge of God's will for us. By now you are beginning to see the benefits of letting go of self will. In Step Eleven you are gently reminded that when you pray for God's will in your life, you are asking for the absolute best solution to whatever you are facing. So often you push and push situations to turn out the way you think you want them to, only to find out that you got second or third or seventh or tenth best. It is a very positive thing to realize that you can trust God to have your best interests at heart. The people, places and things you've given your will over to in the past did not have your best interests at heart. You now trust God enough to say, "Not my will, but thy will be done."

And the power to carry that out. You pray for knowledge of God's will, not just for the sake of having the information, but also for the power to carry it out. Having the information without the willingness or power to carry it out, will not change anything. Having prayed for the knowledge, you listen in meditation for God to tell you the things you need to do. Sometimes a path will open; sometimes God will bring to mind a defect of character that is getting in your way, sometimes God will challenge you in the way you are behaving through intuitive thoughts or feelings you have. Often the power to make the changes God seems to want you to make comes through the people in your support groups. It can even come from seeing someone stuck in old behavior. You can be motivated to change by seeing the consequences others are experiencing because of their unwillingness to act differently. Once having asked for direction and listened for guidance, you can act with assurance, knowing that if you are on the wrong track, you will come to know it. And you always know that you are not alone.

Step Twelve

Having had a spiritual awakening as the result of these steps, we tried to carry this message to others and to practice these principles in all our day-to-day living.

Having had a spiritual awakening as the result of these steps. It is no wonder that an individual who comes to the steps—and in the process of time admits to powerlessness, admits to humanness, admits to the need for a relationship with God, actively pursues that relationship, cleans house, makes amends, and maintains this behavior—has a spiritual awakening. This spiritual awakening is the purpose of working the steps. It is an awakening in which the woman who loves sex addicts discovers she has worth and value, that she is loved by God, and can be loved by others if she will only believe in her lovableness, and open up her heart and let that love in. This awakening to a spiritual connection with a power greater than herself can give her the power to change her way of relating to herself and the world. She can now see herself as a precious child of a loving God, and treat herself and others accordingly.

We tried to carry this message to others. In the beginning of Alcoholics Anonymous, it was not a matter of a drunk alcoholic seeking advice and support from someone who was sober. It was the recovering alcoholic who sought out the active drinker. Bill W., the co-founder of AA, knew that if he couldn't share what he had discovered about his relationship with God and its importance to his sobriety, he wouldn't be able to stay sober. This is true for women who love sex addicts, too. As you progress in your recovery, and become less absorbed in your own pain, you begin to recognize when others around you are in pain.   You will begin to see opportunities to share your experience, strength, and hope with other women who are suffering from the same low self esteem, dependency or independency problems, and lack of boundaries that you experienced.   And you will share, not to get them well, but to remain mindful of the miracle of recovery in your own life. Without constant reminders, you are likely to forget where your strength and health comes from, and become complacent.

One of the truest sayings around recovery groups is, "You can't keep it if you don't give it away." The door to recovery opened to you because others passed this way before. It is your joy, as well as your responsibility, to keep the door open for those who follow, and lead them to the door if they can't find it. It is the only way to insure freedom for all.

And to practice these principles in all our day-to-day living. Here is the most practical part of the Twelve Steps. Take what you have learned, and keep doing it every day. Practice admitting your powerlessness over the problems in your life. Practice acknowledging God's ability to run your life and keep you from practicing old behaviors. Practice new thinking and behavior skills. Practice prayer and meditation. Like the athlete who must exercise daily to stay in good shape, you need to practice daily the new skills you have learned, so you can stay in good emotional and spiritual shape.   It took many years of practicing old behaviors for you to end up with such low self esteem, and such a lack of boundaries. It will take practice to become the new woman you want to be. But it is possible.

25

One Twelve Step Story

The Twelve Steps are, of course, one of the primary tools of the program. Working the steps is essential to growth. Many women who love sex addicts find that, for any given situation, they can, "work the steps on it," and come to some resolution of the problem, whatever that may be. In some cases, it may be as simple as recognizing that they are powerless over a person or situation (Step One). At other times, they may recognize that they haven't asked their higher power into the situation (Step Three). They may see a need for an inventory of the situation, to see what part they're playing in it (Step Four). They may see that they're keeping a secret about themselves that is keeping them sick, and they need to tell someone (Step Five). Perhaps they identify a defect of character they need to eliminate (Steps Six and Seven). They may see that their behavior has harmed themselves or another person, and that they need to make amends (Steps Eight and Nine). Whatever the problem, it is very likely that one of the steps will apply.

The following is how one woman worked the steps in her Co-SA program:

My name is Julie, and I'm a co-sex addict. When I first came to Co-SA meetings, I had no idea what it would mean to "work the steps" in Co-SA. I had been to a different Twelve Step meeting and worked the steps in that program, but really had not admitted my powerlessness over my co-dependency with sex addicts.

It took me several months in the program before I became willing to believe that I had a disease of my own. I began to look at how I responded to being around a sex addict. My boundaries would just disappear. I would find myself agreeing to things I knew I didn't want any part of. Sometimes I would feel really offended by their behavior, but other times I would get almost giddy around them. It was like I was either an ashamed child or a nervous, flirtatious one. And it seemed that I didn't have a choice about my response. It would just happen.

I already knew, consciously at least, that I was powerless over the sex addict and what he was doing. I knew I couldn't be enough for him, or prevent him from acting out in any way. What I didn't know for a long time was that I was powerless over *my* behavior when I was around a sex addict. I would just go on automatic, and be who they wanted me to be, until the point sometime later when I would come to my senses and say, "Why did that happen to me again?" Or I would find myself obsessing about what they did, or what I did, not realizing that I was still trying to figure them out so I could control them. Recognizing powerlessness, as the first step suggests, is the opposite of trying to control.

I would have still denied it back then, but I can see now how unmanageable my life was because of my reaction to sex addicts. This is the second half of Step One—admitting we were powerless over our co-dependency with the sex addict, and that our lives had become unmanageable. I spent a lot of mental and emotional energy on addicts. I spent a lot of mental and emotional energy on trying to be who they wanted me to be. It left me irritable with my children at times. I lost productive time at work because of my obsession. I went to great lengths to look the way I thought they thought I should look, and shamed myself unmercifully for not being good enough. I neglected my own emotional, physical, financial, and spiritual well being in order to connect with a sex addict. I let them define my reality, and would believe them when the real truth was apparent. Most of my decisions were based on what I thought would be best for my relationship with the sex addict, not on what would be best for me and my children.

Today, I know that, of myself, I can't change either the sex addict or the way I react. My reactions were based on my childhood experiences of sexual abuse. They were so ingrained, I was unable to change them, even when I desperately wanted to. Until I really believed I couldn't do it on my own, I wasn't acknowledging my powerlessness and unmanageability.

Fortunately, the program gives me an immediate answer. The second step says, "Came to believe that a power greater than ourselves could restore us to sanity." In Twelve Step programs, insanity is described as doing things the same way over and over, but expecting different results. Lack of sanity for me has come to mean lack of wholeness. Even though I had worked the steps in Al-Anon, I guess I was still, to some extent, looking for my wholeness outside of myself.

It took awhile in the program for me to realize that, as long as I was in any way trying to control other people and my reactions to them, I was not relying on a power greater than myself. As long as I was trying to figure this co-dependency thing out on my own, there was no room for a higher power to act in my life. And for just that long, my behavior around sex addicts stayed the same, and so did the results of my behavior. I had to get tired of things turning out the same way before I was willing to let go of control and recognize that, no matter what I did, it wasn't working.

Emotional pain was what brought me to my knees. I had exhausted everything I knew to do, and my life was still unmanageable. Even when my life looked calm on the surface, my inner life—my self-esteem and emotions—remained in turmoil. It was sort of a final act of desperation. I either had to come to believe that the Higher Power I had come to know in Al-Anon would work in this area too, or have things keep turning out the same way. I chose the Higher Power. I wasn't sure it would work. I wasn't even sure if I really knew how to do it. Program friends told me, as they had in Al-Anon, that all I needed to know was that I didn't have all the answers, and that there was a power greater than me who did.

As I worked the second and third steps in my Co-SA program I realized that, while I had trusted my Higher Power with regard to the alcoholics in my life, trusting where my sexuality was involved was altogether different. My sexuality was badly damaged through childhood sexual abuse at the hands of adults who I was taught to respect and obey. Even my parents, who did not sexually abuse me, did not protect me, although I told them of the abuse.

I did some writing about "God as I understood Him," and saw that I was still carrying in my mind and heart the image of a God who was a combination of my parents: harsh, strict, shaming, and judgmental like Mother, and distant and uninvolved like Dad. It was easy for me to see why it took so long for me to be willing to turn my will and my life over to the care of *that* God, as the Third Step suggests.

I practiced remembering who I believe God to be today: kind, loving, willing to be involved in my life, most certainly trustworthy. It's much easier to turn my will and my life over to the care of a Higher Power who does not look so much like my human parents. And when I do, I am letting go of control. I am acknowledging my willingness to be different. By being willing to have God in control of my life, I have a chance at the wholeness I've been missing. I am being "restored to sanity."

If willingness was all I had to have, there would only be three steps. Beginning with the Fourth Step, I had to take action on my own behalf. I had to look in detail at what I had been doing that wasn't working in my life. I did two Fourth Steps in Al-Anon over the years, but in my Co-SA Fourth Step I made a searching and fearless moral inventory as it related to my relationships with sex addicts. That meant I had to go all the way back to childhood, as I believe that the men who abused me were sex addicts. It wasn't easy. It brought back many painful memories, and a lot of scary feelings. It also showed me how early in my life I learned to try to control not only the addict, but my whole environment, so that I could feel safe. I could see how I never really had any hope of being anything other than what I turned out to be: co-dependent to sex addicts.

I was able to see not only the innocence of the child I had been, but also the devastation I brought about in my adult life as a result of behaviors that had remained essentially unchanged for over thirty years. I looked like an adult, and talked like an adult, but when it came to men in general, and sex addicts in particular, I reverted emotionally back to childhood. As I did when I was being abused, around men I felt shameful, unworthy of love, incapable of taking care of myself, useless unless I could somehow be enough to fill whatever needs they seemed to have.

In order to deal with my feelings of unworthiness, I became a high achiever, a perfectionist, judgmental of myself and anyone else who could not meet my impossibly high standards. I also remained convinced, at some deep level, that the world was unsafe, and I needed someone (a man) to protect me from it. Never mind that they were emotionally abusive or unavailable, and financially irresponsible. I just couldn't bear to be alone.

Probably the most destructive defect of character I found in my Co-SA Fourth Step was not believing in my inherent value. Today I know that, when God created us our value was a given, and could not be changed by outer circumstances, no matter how abusive and shameful. For many, many years I forgot that, and acted out of a feeling of worthlessness. My whole life reflected that sense of shame. I dealt with issues of anger, helplessness, guilt, and shame. It was the most honest appraisal of my behavior that I was capable of. I may uncover more defects of character as I continue to work my program, and I will know how to deal with them.

In the Fifth Step I was able to admit to myself, to the God of my understanding, and to my sponsor, everything I had uncovered in my Fourth Step. I held nothing back, because I knew I wouldn't have full recovery if I did, and I do not want to go back to the way I was.

Having done a Fifth Step twice before, I knew what to expect. My sponsor did not shame me for my past behavior, or tell me what I should do about it now. She simply listened with empathy, and assured me that I am a precious child of God. She affirmed my willingness to grow spiritually, and commented on the growth she could already see in me. There is freedom in sharing yourself with another. It is said, "We are only as sick as the secrets we keep," and I don't want to be sick anymore.

In Step Six, I looked at the behaviors I had been using that I was willing to change. Most of my character defects were merely coping skills I picked up in order to survive my childhood—coping skills that were not only unnecessary, but probably harmful to my life today. Recognizing that I don't need these tools anymore, and being willing to have God remove them, are two different things though. It took some time and effort for me to figure out which ones I was willing to live without.

My inner child frequently felt threatened by the loss of these coping mechanisms, and I felt a lot of inner turmoil about giving some of them up. I had to do a lot of "inner child" work as a part of Steps Six and Seven. For example, when I considered giving up my perfectionism, the child inside of me cried, "No, no we have to be perfect so they will leave us alone." She still believed she could somehow stop the abuse if she was just good enough. I have learned to acknowledge her fear, but act out of the knowledge that stopping the sexual abuse wasn't an option when I was a child, and that it reflected on the abuser and not me. I don't have to be perfect to be valued and respected today.

Over a period of time, I have become willing, most days, to have God remove my perfectionism, and in fact all of the defects of character I identified in Step Four. Again, willingness has been the key. Not just willingness to have them gone, but willingness to replace them with a behavior that is more beneficial to me. Today I am willing to believe, and act out of my belief in my God-given value. As a result, I treat myself and everyone around me with more kindness, love and consideration than I knew I was capable of. Steps Six and Seven were key growth steps for me.

Next, I carried my willingness on to Step Eight, which says, "Made a list of persons we had harmed and became willing to make amends to them all." Again, I had made similar lists in Al-Anon, but the focus of this list was on how my sexual co-addiction had adversely affected me and those around me. The people who wrote the Twelve Steps had a lot of wisdom, putting amends way down near the end of the list. If anyone had told me I would be making amends to my ex-husband, for example, when I was back at Step One feeling victimized, I would have left and not come back. By the time I reached Step Eight though, I was beginning to see the positive effects of honesty in my life. I had let go of much of the shame of the abuse, and liked the lighter feeling I had. I was assured that working Steps Eight and Nine would relive me of any traces of guilt I was still harboring. I was willing.

In making my list, I chose a guideline from the AA program: I looked to see where my instincts and coping mechanisms had gone awry, and had caused physical, mental, emotional, or spiritual damage to others or to myself. I chose to add financial damage to that list as well. It was easy to see that I needed to put myself on the list. My sponsor recommended putting God on the list, for all the times I had played God in my own, and other peoples', lives.

Probably the hardest part was looking at where I had harmed the sex addicts I had been involved with. I had to let go of my victim stance, and acknowledge my part in the difficulties of those relationships. Many times I played the part of their Higher Power, and allowed them to be my Higher Power. This is spiritually damaging. Many, many times I enabled them to continue in their addiction, preventing them from suffering the consequences of their behavior. I was told that any enabling is murder. I realized I had been a party to the continued destruction of their lives. Often I took on their feelings, not allowing them the emotional growth that comes from feeling our own feelings. In my frustration and anger at their unwillingness to change, I gossiped about them to their friends and co-workers. Yes, I could see where my behavior had caused them some harm. I put them on the list.

Making the list was just half the work. I had to become willing to make amends to them *all*. To me, making amends means to be willing to be different. I had to know, inside of me, that I was willing to change the way I had been acting toward myself and all the people on my list. It really helped me when I heard at a meeting that I will know I'm willing when I see that whatever I do to you affects me, too. All the things I did that hurt you, hurt me too. And as I make amends to you for those actions, I'm making amends to me. Today I am determined to be part of the solution, not part of the problem. All these things helped me to be willing to make my amends.

In Step Nine, once again I am asked to take action on my willingness. Step Nine says, "Made direct amends to such people wherever possible, except when to do so would injure them or others." Time and time again, as I have become truly willing, God has provided the opportunity for me to make direct amends. I have opportunity daily to make amends to myself, and the child inside of me, by treating myself as if I believe in my value.

The beauty of it is, the better I treat myself, the more I believe in my value. My self-esteem just grows and grows. I have been provided a setting to make amends to my teenage daughter. For a long time I beat myself up because I didn't make financial amends. Then I realized that for a long time, it wasn't possible. I was a single mother supporting two children, and for many years my low self-esteem kept me in low paying jobs. Today I am in a better position to make those financial amends.

There was a fine line I had to walk when making amends to the sex addicts who had been in my life. As far as I was aware, they were all still practicing their addictions. If I knew where they were and went directly to them, I could be putting myself and my inner child in a potentially abusive situation, and yet I wanted to make the amends. My sponsor and I discussed the best course of action to take in each situation, and I prayed a lot about it. For the amends I have left to make, I just need to stay willing, and trust that my higher power will provide me with the appropriate opportunity.

Step Ten is about maintaining my sanity on a daily basis. It says, "Continued to take personal inventory and when we were wrong, promptly admitted it." If I use the definition of sanity that I used in Step Two, wholeness, it makes it easy for me to take an inventory in the moment, or at the end of my day. To maintain my recovery, I need to respect my wholeness and yours, too.

If I take on your feelings, or suffer your consequences, I have not allowed you to experience your wholeness, or me to experience mine. If I am busy with your feelings and your life, I am not paying attention to my own. If I give a piece of myself away to you, by not saying no when I really mean to, for example, I am not respecting my wholeness. If I people please, I am not respecting my wholeness.

There have been times in my life when I have given so many little bits of myself away in order to please others that there was danger of my disappearing altogether. I am no longer willing to do that to myself. On the other hand, when I demand that you act to my specifications, or resent you when you don't, I have not respected your wholeness. If I manipulate or control situations in an attempt to solicit a particular reaction from you, I have not respected your wholeness.

Recently I noticed my husband had not initiated sex in several days. My first instinct was to initiate something myself, just in case he was trying to see how long it would take me to become interested. I wasn't really feeling sexual, but I didn't want him to think I was not being sexual enough. I thought twice, though, and just went to sleep.

The next day, I brought it up in a meeting and was asked, "Did it ever occur to you to ask him what was going on with him?" Until that moment, talking to him about it never occurred to me. My old behavior of trying to control through manipulation was still my instinctive reaction after all these years in recovery. I'm glad we aim for progress and not perfection in this program. I was able to go home after that meeting and talk to my husband, who had not been sexual for reasons totally different than I suspected. I was able to make amends for not having thought about talking to him in the first place. This is practicing Step Ten in my life.

Step Eleven was a stumbling block for me for awhile. It says, "Sought through prayer and meditation to improve our conscious contact with God, praying only for knowledge of God's will for us and the power to carry that out." Prayer was not a problem. I was willing to pray. What bothered me was meditation. First, I felt that I had to do it right, and everybody I talked to had their own ideas of how to do it. Second, I had a lot of trouble relaxing enough to be in any kind of meditative state. I felt like if I was as relaxed as I needed to be, I wouldn't be able to protect myself if an abuser came along. I just didn't feel safe being that vulnerable.

Once I realized that it was my scared, abused inner child who was wanting to stay tense and hypervigilant, I was able to find a way for her to be comfortable with being relaxed and not constantly on guard. I meditated in a chair, sitting up, covered with a blanket from my childhood. Once I felt safe, meditation became easier. Today, I use my meditation time to read some recovery or spiritual material, and get quiet in my mind to see what God might have to say to me about it.

What about God's will for me? In the beginning I wanted God to put it up in neon lights, so I would be sure to get it. Apparently God doesn't work that way. That's why I need to be willing to listen to that still, small voice within. It takes quieting my usually whirling thoughts, and making room for God's voice. If I start my day with prayer and meditation, and do an inventory of my behavior at the end of the day, I can usually go to sleep at night knowing that however things have turned out is God's will for right now. It doesn't always match what I might have done, but my vision tends to be somewhat limited.

The last step is what keeps this program growing in my heart, and around the world: "Having had a spiritual awakening as the result of these steps, we tried to carry this message to others, and to practice these principles in all our day-to-day living." The spiritual awakening to me was finally recognizing what tremendous value I have in my God's eyes. I realized that I am a spiritual being having a human experience, instead of a human being trying to have a spiritual experience. My God never intended for my life to be unmanageable and unhappy. All I had to do, to turn it around from the mess it was in, was to recognize my importance to God's plan, and be willing to act out of the knowledge that we are all precious. When I remember who I am, and that my value doesn't change because I forget occasionally, it makes it easy for me to practice these principles in my daily life. I am able to treat myself and others as I think God would have me treat us. Life is a lot smoother because of this program.

Carrying the message is what we do when we allow God to work in our lives. It is God who gives me the right words to say to a woman reaching out for help and understanding. It is God who gives me the strength to try new behaviors that support my value and the value of those around me. If someone admires my serenity, or growth, or self-esteem, it is because I was willing to give up control of my life to a Higher Power. It's not me that makes my life attractive, it's God working through me.

The message of this program is: God loves us all, and it works, if you work it. I provided honesty, open-mindedness and willingness, and God did the rest. I am grateful.

26

Further Recovery Options

In addition to the vital attendance and involvement in Twelve Step recovery, many women who love sex addicts benefit greatly from professional therapy.

"What? Am I in need of therapy too?" you might be asking yourself if the idea of therapy frightens you. "Am I crazy, or what?" A general discussion of the types of therapy, and treatment settings available might help you decide if therapy is for you.

Like the medical or financial fields, the mental health field has various levels of professionally trained people. These professionals have a wide variety of philosophies and training perspectives, and can meet different needs of women who love sex addicts.

Psychiatrist

Psychiatrists are medical doctors. They attend several years of medical school, and are trained to look at biological reasons for problems with the human being. They will be trained in medications that influence the chemistry of the brain. This professional would be of real help or support to the woman who loves sex addicts if she has been previously diagnosed with a a disorder of depression, manic-depression, or other problem that requires the supervision of a medical doctor. He or she can prescribe medication the woman might need to feel better, such as anti-depressant medication.

Often a psychiatrist offices with other mental health professionals who do individual, or group therapy. If the psychiatrist has had addiction training, or has had exposure to Patrick Carnes' training for the professional who works with sex addicts, he or she may be of some help to you as you work on your issues. Please refer to the resource listing in the appendix for Del Amo Hospital, which keeps a listing of psychiatrists who have received sexual addiction training.

Psychologist

A psychologist is quite different from a psychiatrist, although they are often confused as they both have the designation of doctor. Psychologists are Ph.D, Ed.D, or Psy D.'s, *not* medical doctors. They cannot prescribe medication. They spend their educational training looking at the cognitive, or thinking, aspects of the human being, such as I.Q., reading/math levels, psychological testing, and the like. He or she is often trained to do individual, group, and marital therapy.

Psychologists with a Doctorate in Psychology can be of great help to the woman who loves a sex addict, especially if they have had experience working with the sex addict, or general addiction population. If you choose a psychologist you can again refer to the Del Amo Hospital listing in the appendix. They can refer you to a local Ph.D. who has had training in the area of sexual addiction and sexual co-addiction.

A psychologist can be of help in therapy to a sexual co-dependent especially if the co-dependent is experiencing any psychological disorder, such as depression, suicidal thoughts, or a compulsive eating, sleeping, or drinking disorder. Often these survival mechanisms respond well to treatment under the care of a trained and licensed psychologist.

Licensed Professional Counselor

The Licensed Professional Counselor, or LPC, usually has either masters level training, or PH.D. level training with expertise in another field; i.e., Sociology or Anthropology. They can acquire a counselor's license through taking certain counseling classes. A masters level degree is the minimum required for the LPC in most states. The masters level professional may also have a degree in an area other than counseling, like an M.Ed. (Masters in Education), and take ten to fifteen classes in counseling during or after his or her graduate degree program, to acquire a professional license from the state he or she practices in. This is something to note in your interview with a Licensed Professional Counselor. You can ask exactly what their background is, because a license does not require a full degree in counseling in some states. This can be important for the woman who loves sex addicts to know when she is seeking help for her own issues or for the issues surrounding her family, marriage or children.

The masters level LPC, much like a psychologist, can be a great resource for a woman as she deals with family and individual problems. An LPC is usually able to identify and deal with depression, obsessive/compulsive disorders, addictive disorders, co-dependency, and other issues such as anorexia or bulimia. LPC's, like psychiatrists and psychologists, have ongoing training and, in most states, will have a more reasonable fee structure for those seeking counseling. In finding a Licensed Professional Counselor, ask how many years they have been practicing, and review the "Questions to Ask" section at the end of this chapter, to determine the counselor's experience with sexual addiction or with women who love sex addicts.

Social Workers

Social workers will have either a bachelors or a masters level education. They may have several levels of certification which can differ from state to state. They may be a Certified Social Worker (CSW) or a masters level Social Worker (MSSW), depending on their experience. Their training is mostly from a social perspective. Seeing issues from a social perspective is beneficial, and can be helpful, but unless specific training is given to the Social Worker in the field of addictions, there may be limits as to how helpful they can be.

However, if there is a need for social services for the family or for the addict—for example, in finding places for residential treatment—a Social Worker can usually be quite helpful. In some states the Social Worker is much like a Licensed Professional Counselor, as they do a lot of therapy. In other states they do social histories and things of that nature. In finding a Social Worker, you need to find out what training and experience they have had. You may find that this will be a very beneficial relationship to you, as you seek help for either your own issues, family issues, or the issues of the sex addict. Again, refer to the "Questions to Ask" section.

Pastoral Counselors

Pastoral counseling is also available in many areas. Pastoral Counselors include people who have professional degrees in Counseling from an accredited seminary or institution. They may have a doctoral level education (Ph.D.), or they may have masters level education. Pastors of local congregations would be included in this category, although these may have a bachelors level education, or no education at all. Such counselors can be significantly helpful to those who have strong church, Christian, or religious backgrounds. Pastoral Counselors can be very helpful in your recovery, because development of spirituality is a significant part of recovery for the whole person.

The strengths of a Pastoral Counselor would include his spiritual training, coupled with professional experience and professional training in the fields of addictions, or counseling and psychological training. With such training, a Pastoral Counselor could be of the utmost benefit.

Some possible weaknesses of the Pastoral Counselor might be a lack of training or skill in some areas. The pastor who has had no training in counseling may be of brief support to the woman who is in a relationship with a sex addict, but might not be as beneficial in resolving personal issues or identifying other psychological problems that a woman might have, including those she might have had prior to being in a relationship with a sex addict.

The Pastoral Counselor, like all other professionals discussed, should be asked the appropriate questions from the "Questions to Ask" section. This is very important. Often, their understanding of addictions and sexual issues can influence how therapeutic they can be to you.

Christian Counseling

Christian counseling is another form of counseling which is now readily available in most larger cities, as well in some smaller communities. Christian counseling is not exactly the same as pastoral counseling. Many Christian counselors will not hold a position as a Pastor, nor will they have professional pastoral counselor training, or continuing education requirements.

A Christian counselor is often professionally trained in the theory of counseling, psychology and human development. These counselors can be masters or doctoral level trained individuals, but the training that any counselor receives can vary widely. It is wise to check the Christian counselor's training prior to having any therapeutic relationship.

There is a specific benefit in having a Christian counselor for those who embrace the Christian faith. They can be a great source of help, especially if they are able to integrate Biblical truths and Biblical understanding into the healing process. They can be very supportive and encouraging to the personal development of the woman who loves sex addicts, and they can also facilitate growth for the whole family, or in the relationship between the woman and the sex addict she loves. Again, ask the questions relating to training and expertise in the area of sexual addiction.

Certified Alcohol And Drug Addiction Counselors (CADAC) Or Licensed Chemical Dependency Counselors (LCDC)

CADAC's and LCDC's are available in most areas, although their designations may differ from state to state. These are counselors with a variety of training backgrounds. They may have a Ph. D., a masters or bachelors degree, or may have had no formal education whatsoever. Again, the training of an individual counselor is very significant. This cannot be stressed more than in the field of alcohol and drug addictions. In some states, individuals recovering from alcoholism or drug addiction who want to enter the helping profession find that such certification is the easiest way into this field. They do have a valid experience and understanding of the addiction process, as well as understanding of the recovery process. However, caution must be used, in that recovering people often have multiple addiction problems. This is something to be noted when interviewing an addictions counselor. In addition, it is important to ask how they have integrated a Twelve Step philosophy into their own lives. Our personal opinion is that unless a counselor has done at least a Fourth and Fifth step and has begun the process of making amends, his or her perceptions might still be clouded by guilt and shame, and the counselor might not be able to facilitate the growth you need in your life.

Addictions counselors do have some strengths, however. They are often trained in family systems theory. They are familiar with the dynamics of addiction, about which you will need much information. They also usually come from a Twelve Step perspective. Often these counselors can be found in alcohol and drug addiction treatment centers, both in-patient and out-patient. Sometimes they are in an office with a psychiatrist, psychologist, masters level counselor or, an LPC. They are often supervised in their work by a degreed professional. You can ask if the person's case load is being supervised, and by whom, and what that supervision process is. This is important because some supervisors, due to time constraints, will not review each case thoroughly. Another benefit to an addictions counselor is that he or she would be aware of recovery groups in the area, and the importance of support groups in the recovery process.

Marriage And Family Counselors

Marriage and Family counselors can have a variety of degrees in education also. They may have a Ph.D., or a masters degree in marriage and family counseling. For the woman who loves sex addicts, this may or may not be helpful, depending on her situation. If you are in a marriage or a committed relationship, such a counselor can be very beneficial.

Marriage and Family counselors come from a family systems approach, taking into consideration the needs of the entire family, and not just the needs of one person. Also, they will be highly attuned to how each family member processes problems, and how the family members interact with each other.

For example, in some addictive systems the addict is the one who is perceived as needing help, the wife is the one who is strong and "helps" the addict, while the children are her supporters, or her cheerleaders in helping Dad. From a systems approach, a counselor might look at this situation and say, "Dad needs to be sick so that Mom can be a helper. Mom needs to give up the helper role and establish her own identity and boundaries, so if Dad recovers the family doesn't need somebody else to be sick; i.e. the children or Mother herself.

The marriage and family counselor will be highly astute in these matters and can be beneficial to the woman who loves sex addicts, as well as to the family as a whole. Refer to the "Questions to Ask" section to determine what training and experience this counselor has in addictions in general, and in sexual addiction specifically, as well as in recovery from sexual addiction.

It is very appropriate to interview the professional you are considering as a therapist. Each woman has a different history, and could have possible conflicts with certain professionals due to her past experiences. Also, the many professionals discussed here represent a sort of continuum of care. At one point in recovery you might find one certain type of professional more helpful than another. Many practices include several types of therapists, and are able to treat women who love sex addicts from what is known as a multi-disciplinary view. In interviewing a potential therapist, consider the following list of questions.

Questions to Ask

- Do you have experience working with sex addicts?
- How many sex addicts have you seen in the last two months?
- Do you have training to do therapy with people with addictions? (State or Board certification?)
- Are you a recovering person working a Twelve Step program?
- What books have you read on sexual addiction?

- Have you ever treated just the wife/partner of a sex addict?
- Do you have specific training to deal with (if these issues apply to you) rape victims, survivors of child sexual abuse, incest or other trauma?

The Treatment Setting

You could be quite alarmed to realize there are so many different types of training and professionals in the mental health field. This is a positive situation, though, given the complexity of human beings. The intricacies of human relationships often require professionals trained in different areas and at different levels of education for treatment to be the most effective. This issue can be confusing, but if you are given the right information, you will be able to make a better choice in selecting a therapist.

The choice of an appropriate treatment setting is also significant for the woman who loves sex addicts. Treatment settings available to you will vary considerably depending upon your location. Rural areas might present limited choices. Larger metropolitan areas will offer most types of treatment settings. In addition to private facilities you can also check into what community and state resources are available. We will talk about each of these as they relate to the woman who loves sex addicts, because one setting can be more appropriate or beneficial than another. Again, it will depend on your particular history and needs.

Out-patient Setting

In an out-patient setting, you go to see a professional counselor of some degree, including any of those previously mentioned. In this setting you may be asked to come once, twice, or up to three times per week, usually for about 45 minutes to an hour per session. In these sessions you will discuss, and share your feelings about what is going on in your life and in your relationships. You will get the benefit of the experience and training of the professional you are seeing.

This is by far the least restrictive treatment environment, and can be most therapeutic in that it does not disrupt your lifestyle more than a couple of hours each week. In most cases a therapist will require some homework, so you will need to plan an extra hour or so a week to do any writing or reading your therapist suggests. Couples can also receive marriage counseling on an out-patient basis, which might be once or twice a week. Children can have therapy once or twice during the week as well. Remember, the whole family has probably been affected by the dysfunction of sexual addiction.

Out-patient therapy can be particularly beneficial for those whose dysfunction does not greatly impair their day-to-day lives. Another prerequisite for success in an out-patient setting is a high degree of motivation. If an individual is highly motivated to identify and deal with issues that surface, and is willing to process the pain and experience the feelings connected with past and present life situations, this setting can be very, very therapeutic. Patients who are highly motivated, and do the homework that they are asked to do, often find great relief in this treatment setting.

The out-patient therapy can take place in a private professional's office, in a mental health clinic, a community service agency, or through a state or county counseling service. The cost will vary depending upon the training of the counselor and the agency, and can range anywhere from $25.00 to $125.00 per hour. Out-patient therapy is the most cost effective treatment for most people. Generally, a portion of the costs may be covered by your health insurance.

Partial Hospitalization

The next level of treatment, as far as intensity is concerned, is called Partial Hospitalization or Day Treatment. In this setting, clients commute to a state, community, or private psychiatric hospital. They generally attend daily sessions— usually from 8 or 9 a.m. until 4 or 5 p.m.—during which time clients participate in various types of groups on such topics as self-esteem, assertiveness training, communications skills, family systems, stress reduction, psychological trauma, process groups, and recreational therapy. Partial hospitalization provides a well rounded approach to therapy. It is beneficial for those who need more than mere out-patient therapy, but who do not need to be confined to a hospital. Medical insurance may also cover a part of the services provided by a Partial Hospitalization program.

Day treatment is more costly and more time consuming than out-patient treatment, as well as more intense. You can accomplish a lot of work in this setting, while still maintaining your life at home. In this setting, you will be seen by a psychiatrist, you will have medical supervision, and you may have psychological testing done to see if there are other psychological issues that need to be addressed. In addition, you will probably have an individual therapist who will see you one to three times per week at the hospital. Bonding with this therapist can ease the eventual transition from partial hospitalization into an out-patient setting, where you can continue your growth in relationship with this person. This is beneficial to your long term recovery.

This setting can be an emotional boot camp experience for the woman who loves sex addicts. The amount of support she receives is great, and she will be encouraged to attend Twelve Step support group meetings outside the facility. Often the day treatment will focus on a Twelve Step recovery approach.

To find out if a particular program will be beneficial to you, ask if they have addiction programs, and specifically programs that treat sexual addiction or co-sexual addiction. If you are fortunate enough to find one of this nature, it can be highly beneficial to you.

In approaching partial hospitalization, ask any questions that pertain to your particular issues, such as childhood sexual abuse or rape. Also, ask the person arranging your admission to assign you to a doctor who has experience currently, or very recently, in addiction or sexual addiction treatment. Finally, ask about payment arrangements. Often these institutions will have an administrative allowance that can relieve you of some of the additional expenses.

In-patient Setting

The in-patient setting is the most intense and most restrictive environment. In this setting you live at the institution for the entire length of your stay, perhaps twenty, thirty, or up to sixty days, depending on your personal issues and needs. Length of stay can also be affected by your insurance coverage, which may set certain limits on this kind of care.

In an in-patient setting, you will be exposed to all of the things that the partial hospital setting provides. In addition to receiving twenty-four hour nursing care, you will attend classes on communication, assertiveness, trauma, stress reduction, Twelve Step recovery, addictions, recreational therapy and exercise.

The enclosed environment can be very beneficial for you as a woman who loves sex addicts in that your own personal issues will surface more quickly. In this setting you will be exposed to yourself more readily because you have no place to retreat, to build your walls back up. All of your time and energy can be directed toward healing. If the institution is adequately prepared, and the staff is adequately trained, you will make significant progress.

In an in-patient setting, as in partial hospitalization, you will be assigned a medical doctor, a psychiatrist, and often will receive psychological testing. You will also be assigned a counselor of some level or degree. This could be an addictions counselor, a licensed professional counselor or perhaps a social worker, or even a Ph.D. When seeking in-patient care, it is wise to discuss with the hospital, right up front, the qualifications of the people you will be treated by while in the hospital. In the private sector, financial arrangements should also be negotiated prior to admission. Often, if your medical insurance covers a large portion, say 70%, 80%, or 90% of the charges, the hospital may have an administrative allowance which can absolve you of the remaining 10% to 30%. Get these arrangements in writing up front if you go into an in-patient setting.

Due to changes in the insurance industry, it may be more difficult to get approval for treatment in this setting. The criteria for in-patient admission can include depression or suicidal ideation. In a relationship with a sex addict there can be extreme moments of desperation, and these must be honestly acknowledged by the woman who loves a sex addict. If you are feeling extremely depressed, are having thoughts such as, "Why go on?" or, "I wish I wasn't here," or "There is a gun in the closet," or even more likely, "There are some pills in the medicine cabinet," you are a candidate for in-patient treatment.

Indeed, this is the ideal setting for someone who has been brought to the end of her rope, and who really needs a safe place where she can regain her strength and her emotional well-being. In-patient treatment is a place where she can better learn to face relationships and life on life's terms. This setting can be an extremely positive experience for the woman who loves a sex addict.

27

The Therapeutic Experience

Recovery is very positive for the woman who loves sex addicts, but it can also be one of the most painful, heart wrenching experiences that she will ever have. In her therapy experience she will be asked to look at things which she has not looked at before. She will be asked to look at her rationalizations for her own behavior, and how they impact her relationship with her husband or partner. She will need to examine her methods of control, her technique of manipulating her husband or lover, her lack of assertiveness, and her lack of communication skills. She will also need to examine her inability to be emotionally vulnerable, her need to be perfect and make everything look okay to others, and her need to make sure nobody finds out about this deep secret that she is keeping, or finds out that her marriage isn't what she's been pretending it was. She is going to be asked why she is in this relationship, and why she continues in it. While this can be very painful, it can also be very enlightening.

She will be asked to look at any rapes, childhood sexual abuse, molestation, homosexual, or bestiality experiences that may have happened to her. She will have to look into any shameful experiences that she has had, as well as any traumas associated with divorce or the death of a loved one. She will have to consider her whole life history at some point, evaluate any unresolved pain, and be willing to experience that pain. She must be willing to reopen these events and walk through them in a healthier manner.

For the first time in her life perhaps, the woman will be asked to consider her own needs, and be able to find some means of meeting those needs. She may be asked why she is in a dependent relationship where she has no say in her own life, and what is she avoiding by staying in such a relationship? She will be forced to look at the issue of responsibility, and discover why she hasn't taken the initiative to be responsible for herself.

A co-sex addict in recovery may be challenged on parenting issues, and have to acknowledge the effects of her own and her spouse's behavior on her children. These can be extremely painful issues to look at, especially for the woman who is carrying a heavy load of shame, guilt, and embarrassment, as most women who love sex addicts are.

If you are a woman who loves a sex addict, some questions are probably surfacing right now. "Oh my God, why do I have to experience all of that?" you may be asking. "Why do I have to look at all of those things? Why, why, why?"

When you look at these issues with the help of a therapist, you will find the anger, rage, and humiliation that you have experienced, but not been able to express. Underneath all the pain, though, you will find a love for yourself that you didn't realize was there. You will develop the ability to say no when you want to say no, and yes when you want to say yes. The freedom to make positive choices can be found, as well as the joy of having a positive relationship with someone who knows your secret, and who loves you anyway.

Your therapist will be a cheerleader in your life, and will support your search for fulfillment of the dreams that you have squelched before. You can see these dreams come true as a result of the work you do in therapy and Twelve Step support groups. You will identify the issues that are affecting your life, and address them; you will be able to dissolve sick patterns of relating to and choosing men who want to sexually abuse you, or who are primarily sexually motivated toward you. Therapy can change your lifestyle of sick relationships, and move you into positive female/female relationships as well as positive male/female relationships. You will develop a higher awareness of spirituality, and the role it plays in your life.

These gifts of recovery can be received in the process of therapy, and by attending support group meetings. You will be able to see, finally, what your issues are. Each woman who loves a sex addict, whether she has loved only one or loved many, will need to be willing to address those issues and find in her heart the courage to change. She will begin to believe that she is worthy of having a happy relationship, a happy life, a happy family, and a happy future. If you find the courage in your heart, therapy can be a most positive experience.

Landmarks in Recovery

There are several major landmarks in the therapeutic experience for the woman who loves sex addicts, and we want to review some of these for those of you who will be walking this path. As you walk the path of recovery, we want you to be able to say, "Hey, I've been down that block. I can see that I have reached a significant marker here."

One of you first tasks is identifying that there is a problem. For some women this can take twenty to forty years. For others this may take only months. Identifying the problem *is* a landmark. It happens when you stop rationalizing that you are not giving him enough sex, or you are not good enough, or that you are responsible for his irrational behavior, and understand that you are responsible for believing the lies he has been telling you. You will be able to identify things that are not true, and there will be a new understanding that the problem is not all you. This is a major, major, major landmark. We hope that you have been able to come to this landmark in reading these pages, because it is in identifying the problem that you choose the path to recovery.

Once you have chosen the path, if you continue to walk with courage and with supportive friends, you can achieve a more satisfying lifestyle.

A second major landmark in recovery, as we talked about in Twelve Step programs, is recognizing powerlessness: powerlessness over him; powerlessness over your own internal battles; powerlessness over the rationalizations; powerlessness over the fear, guilt and anger; powerlessness over the shame. You must give up the belief that you can control it any longer. This is a tremendous landmark that is often seen in the early stages of recovery. The depth at which this seed is planted will probably foretell the quality of emotional sobriety that you will have, and the quality of recovery you will achieve. Once you recognize what you are powerless over, you can turn your energies to what you do have power over: changing yourself. That is why you are seeing a therapist in the first place: you need help in changing yourself.

The ability to establish boundaries is another major landmark. You will become able to say no, and able to identify your own needs. This is a landmark which says, "I am worthy," and a point where you cross over from the old beliefs like, "I am not good enough; I am damaged goods. I have been raped. I have been abused. I have been neglected. I have been abandoned. This is the only person who ever loved me. It is the only person who will ever love me."

Instead, you come to a place where you decide, "Hey, I love me. God loves me. That's two. I am okay. I have needs. I need relationships. I need affirming. I need non-sexual touch. I need non-sexual language. I need to realize that I am a person and I will not tolerate being treated as an object." This is a major step of growth, and your therapist will support you in realizing it.

Another large marker in recovery is the willingness to attend support groups. When you attend them, you benefit by learning from, and encouraging, others. Attending support groups on a regular basis can only enhance your recovery for it says, "I am worth getting better. I am worth listening to these stories. I am worth hearing other ways of thinking. I am worth working the Steps. I am worth changing my life. I am worth having a better future." So, it is a landmark which says, "I am committed to a better life. I am committed to *me*."

There is another landmark which is ongoing, and can probably be broken down into many smaller achievements. It is the personal growth that will be evident when you are able to say, "Hey, here is an issue," and work through it. You minimize your suffering as a result of that issue. You do not allow yourself to be set up in the same way. You no longer hear the same rationalizations and believe them. The ability to recognize issues before they cause problems is growth, and the woman who continues on this path of personal recovery will probably be much happier than in her previous lifestyle.

Therapy is an extremely beneficial process. We could write a whole book on personal landmarks in therapy, and still not cover all of them. We hope that you experience the ones we have listed here, and more, as you deal with past and current issues, and as you face your own "defects of character." As they suggest in Twelve Step programs, removing these defects of character insures continued growth for each person in recovery.

The Family and Treatment

We have talked a lot about the individual woman who loves sex addicts, but as the very title suggests, there is her relationship with a sex addict, or sex addicts, as well as with parents, children, and possibly even grandchildren, to consider. When you begin therapy, you need to ask, "How do I get help for not only myself, but for the others who are involved in my life?" Previously, we reviewed a list of professionals who treat women who love sex addicts. There are professionals who have expertise in marital and family problems as well, and those who treat the sex addict himself. Any professional person who has had experience in treating sexual addiction would probably be successful in treating the husband or boyfriend who is a sex addict.

There are also support groups for the sex addict, such as Sex Addicts Anonymous, Sexaholics Anonymous and Sex and Love Addicts Anonymous. These groups can be found by looking in the white pages of the telephone book, or by calling your local Council on Alcohol and Drug Abuse or a psychiatric hospital which keeps a list of the support groups in your area. Such groups can be extremely helpful to the addict. If he chooses to get help, and chooses to get a sponsor and work the Steps, he can get well.

Often, though, he will need professional help too. His issues are life-long; they started the need for dealing with emotions through the use of sex. A man must identify these needs and be able to find alternative ways to meet them. He must learn to "de-objectify" his partner, and move into a new perception of her. These skills can often be learned by the sex addict in therapy. We encourage you to review the list of Questions to Ask before finding someone who can help the sex addict.

What about the marriage? How can that ever work? There are many dynamics that only occur between the sex addict and the co-sex addict, and unless confronted in a therapy session these will be ongoing, even though both partners are getting better individually. Marital counseling can be very effective in dealing with the relationship dynamics of sexual and co-sexual addiction. The most therapeutic situation possible is one in which a woman is getting individual therapy, and her partner is getting individual therapy, and they are also receiving marital therapy on a regular basis. The marital counselor you choose would need to have access to information on the individual growth of each person, and also have experience in the sexual addiction field. This type of counseling can also facilitate personal growth, because often your greatest issues of denial, rationalization and anger come up in marital therapy.

In marital therapy, a couple can learn life long skills of relating. They can learn how to be intimate, how to support one another, allow each other space, respect, self-esteem, and boundaries. Marital therapy may be essential for couples who want to stay together. This is not, however, a guarantee that the damage is repairable. There must be a note of caution here that sometimes, due to the sexual addiction of the man and to the amount of abuse and trauma that have been imposed on the woman, some relationships may not be repairable. Marital counseling will probably identify if this is the case.

Another question you might ask is, "What if he won't go to therapy? What if he is not committed to the relationship?" In a boyfriend/girlfriend relationship, this is easier. You stop seeing him. Actually, this sounds easy, but for many women who love sex adicts, one of the most difficult things to do is to let go of a relationship in which you are getting many of your self-esteem and affirmation needs met. That is why a support group is so important. If he is not committed to personal recovery, it is hard for any relationship to work, because he will continue to operate off sick patterns of thinking, which produce sick behaviors, compulsive patterns, and a selfish lifestyle. This is guaranteed if the sex addict is not getting any help. He is staying the same at the very least, and is probably getting worse.

For the woman who is married to a sex addict, this raises another whole set of questions. We should discuss a process here that doesn't automatically assume, "OK, he is not going to get better, so I am out of here. Goodbye, goodbye, nice seeing you, nice living with you, nice having your kids, send the support." There should be a process that says, "If he won't go, you go. You get better for yourself. You are going to need strength if there is going to be a divorce or separation in the future. You are going to need good friends, understanding and very often you are going to need financial assistance. Give yourself time in this process, and give him time. Go to your meetings, do what is good for you." The family systems approach says that if one person in the family system is changing, it can bring about change in other family members. This is not a guarantee, but at least you will be changing. When you are stronger, you can draw the boundaries as you wish. The support of a professional or a sponsor in drawing these new boundaries can be invaluable.

A healthy separation has been helpful for some recovering sex addict/co-addict relationships. In such a case, the couple decides not to discuss divorce as a first option, but rather to take a period of time, whether it be one, three, or six months, away from each other, living in separate places. This allows them to focus on their own issues and to let healing come to the relationship. Time can heal some of the wounds that have left both partners feeling fragmented. Such a separation gives the man an opportunity to suffer pain and loneliness. Loneliness is often more painful for the addict than anything he can experience, and can help motivate him into a proper perspective of recovery, and a proper perspective of you.

As you draw the boundaries of a healthy separation, they probably need to be written down. Each person should know what the expectations and limitations are. Are you going to date? Are you going to talk on the telephone? How are you going to work with the kids? Who will pay the bills? Are you going to have sex? Such questions must be considered ahead of time to make a separation really successful and therapeutic.

Separation is a healthy alternative to immediate divorce. During the separation, the woman continues to get help, and continues to grow stronger. She begins to deal with her own issues so that, in the case of a legal separation or divorce, she is more able to handle life on life's terms. She won't be going from a very sick relationship directly into a divorce. That could be traumatic and overwhelming for some women.

You may still be asking, "So what if we separate and he still won't get help. What do I do then? What if he uses it as an excuse to act out more? What if he chooses his addiction over me and the kids?" The reality of that is, it was always a possibility while you were married, and will remain a strong possibility until he decides to get help. In such a case, there is probably no answer that will be right for any two women. Each individual has her own belief system, her own values, her own religious convictions, and her own attitudes toward divorce. Each family has its own separate set of needs. Each child must be considered individually. Each woman must consider her support structure, her own personal health, and what it is going to take to see a divorce through. Seek the support of those who know you: your therapist, members of your support group, your pastor, and those who care the most about you. They will be able to give you a perspective on yourself that will assist you in making this kind of decision. They will walk with you through the process, whatever you choose.

Therapy for your children may become necessary. It is essential that they see a professional if you suspect they have been sexually abused. Look at the list of possible ways children can be abused, and decide if they might have suffered any of those listed. If you have an individual therapist, he or she may be able to recommend someone who deals specifically with children. Again, you could call the Golden Valley Health Center listed in the appendix for a referral to a professional in your area. It is our experience that they have the most comprehensive list of professionals who work with families of sex addicts. Remember, you cannot live with a sex addict and not be affected in some way. As you get healthier, your children will learn new coping skills that you model, but they may need the additional support of their own therapist.

28

Letters of Hope

The following are letters written to the readers of this book from co-sex addicts who have been working a recovery program for some time. It is our hope that these letters will encourage you as you begin your recovery, and as you work through the painful issues that have been a part of your past. Recovery is a process, and there will be times for everyone that are wonderful, as well as times that are difficult. If you are open to all your experiences, you can see that no matter what they are, they lead to growth.

Dear Friend,

I watched a new person come in to the Co-SA meeting the other day. I could read her face, and I remembered all those feelings. First the terror of my environment. I believed I was the only one who loved my husband, and yet was afraid to leave the children alone with him for fear he would abuse them. I could barely hold on to both of those thoughts and not go crazy.

I remembered the fear that people would find out and "make" me leave him. Fear that someone would find out, and say it was my fault, and "make" me stay.

I had a lot of anger in the beginning too. I was angry that this had happened to me, angry that "he" had done this to me. Angry that God had done this to me.

I was sad. On some level I knew this was the beginning of the end. I knew that life would never be the same, and that I would have to change.

I felt shame. I was a terrible person. I could not let people close to me because of all of the secrets I kept. I was not worthy of a decent life. I had blown it.

Most of what I felt was numb. I was on constant overwhelm. I could not process all this information and therefore I would stay in a fog. Many times I had to ask someone why I was there, and they would have to tell me my story again. Now I believe the fog was a safety net to keep me from committing suicide.

One of the most comforting words in the Twelve Steps is "we". It truly means you do not have to do this on your own.

There will be someone who has been through what you are experiencing. The more I hear other people's stories, the more I hear my own story. Sometimes the circumstances are different, but most times the feelings are the same.

Meetings are not a place to bash men. Meetings are not a place for all women to get divorced. Meetings are not a place to learn how to make that relationship work. Meetings are a place to learn that we are people who are lovable and capable of giving love. They are a place to develop a relationship with a Higher Power who wants the best for us. Through working the steps, we learn to trust our Higher Power and follow our own path, not a path dictated by another human being. We learn how to parent ourselves, how to love ourselves, how to grow and change and lose the rigid walls we have struggled to maintain. Above all, we learn how to breathe.

I would like to encourage you to attend Co-SA meetings. There are not many places where we can talk about sex, abuse, feelings, and life on such an honest level. Use the meetings to talk as honestly as you can. If you are angry, say so. Be specific. If you are scared, say so. If you feel like dirt, say so, and listen as the people there tell you that you have made some mistakes, but you are not a mistake. Take in the warm glow of these people loving you. Soon you will be able to love yourself. Co-SA is one of life's rare opportunities to love and be loved. Take advantage of it.

Dear Co-SA,

Yesterday, I heard someone say at a meeting, "Anyone living in a sex addict relationship should leave that relationship. It is dangerous to be in an S.A. relationship because of all the venereal diseases and most of all because of the AIDS virus. It is a sick relationship that can't be changed and you had best get out of it."

I was uncomfortable with those statements. I was upset, and driving home I realized why I was so upset. The statements were rigid, judgmental, and sick. I do not have the right to judge my situation by other people's situations. Every situation is different. I do not have the right to judge my decisions by another's beliefs or standards. The woman who was speaking was judging me. That has been my problem: listening and accepting the standards of others as gospel, while rebelling inside, and knowing these standards made me uncomfortable, without knowing why.

In order not to be in a co-addictive relationship with anyone, I would have to run away to a deserted island, where I would not see, hear or converse with another human being for the rest of my life. That is isolation, and I can even do that right here in my own home. I choose not to run away. I choose to find the cracks, the broken thought patterns, all the imperfections in myself and those in my relationship that I have contributed, and find a way to heal or repair them to the best of my ability.

I will not leave my spouse, who has been a non-practicing sex addict for six to nine years. He is just now grasping the ideals of his program. He reminds me of a flower (in slow motion) just starting to break out of the soil. I cannot judge him, I cannot punish him. I can only watch his actions and from them decide what is best for me. Only I know what is best for me. Only I know if I am in a life threatening situation.

This does not mean that everyone is to do as I do. Every situation is different. There are situations where it is best to leave. Only the person in that relationship can decide what is best for them. I accept your right to choose and will support you in your decision.

Yesterday, as soon as I got home, I called a Co-SA friend. I reached out for help, I talked about how I felt, the good qualities my husband has, our situation, etc. My friend said, "It sounds like you are standing up for your husband." I said, "No, I am standing up for myself." She said, "Good for you."

In the last twenty-six years my husband and I have faced and surmounted many obstacles. We have been in the process of remolding our characters, our beliefs, and our love for each other and passing on our experiences to our children, our grandchildren and anyone who comes to us for advice. It is going to take more than twenty-six years to correct those first twenty-six years of dysfunction. I want to stay and see how the story ends.

Finding help in Co-SA has helped me to realize that our old interactions were unhealthy, and that we both have recovery work to do. I didn't know if we could do it over the long haul, so

I took the idea of "One Day at a Time" and started out with the thought, "Today, I won't get a divorce. Today I won't run away." I have choices now that I didn't have then.

Today, I have found the courage to speak up and take care of myself. By doing this, it causes a chain reaction in my relationship with my husband, my children, and everyone who touches my life.

I can only tell you that these things worked for me. They might help you and they might not. It is your situation and your decision.

I have to give others the right to be as sick as I have been, and to find their own way in recovery. I owe them the freedom to choose, to decide what is best for them, to learn in their own way, and to cherish their efforts the way you cherish a baby's first step, first word, first smile, and give them a hug and say, "Good for you!"

Dear Co-SA,

I've been in the program for about a year. I started after I was in treatment for sexual abuse issues. After I left treatment I started dating a sex addict who was emotionally and physically abusive. It wasn't until I started attending meetings and got a sponsor that I was able to set boundaries with this man, and finally get him out of my life.

When my friend asked me what I would say to newcomers, or women who were considering going to meetings and trying to change, I wanted to say something really positive. Instead, what I want to tell you is this: whenever you think you have everything under control, the bottom falls out. But, if you hang in there, go to meetings, talk to other people in the program and above all believe in yourself and your value, you can get better.

Today, I am dating a kind, loving man who lets me be me. I know more about who I want to be. I've gone back to school full time to get a degree, so I can better provide for my son and myself. Three years ago I wouldn't have thought it would be possible. Even one year ago I wouldn't have guessed where I'd be today.

Whatever is going on in your life, there is hope for you. The road is not always smooth, but having friends in Co-SA has sure made the bumps a little easier to take.

Love,

Debbie

Dear Precious Child,

You are a precious child, you know. You always have been. You probably just didn't know it. Well, I'm here to tell you that no matter what your past has been like, no matter how messed up you are today, your future can be better. I am living proof of that.

I struggled a lot with believing in my value when I first came to Co-SA. I would intellectually say, "Of course I know I'm special and precious." The problem is, my heart didn't believe it. The little abused girl inside of me said, "No way. Nobody believes I'm precious, least of all you." And she was talking to the adult me.

In my recovery, I've done a lot of visualization and talking to my inner child. She was there every time I made a bad choice about men, and she needed to find out she could trust me again. Slowly, with lots of care and attention, she is beginning to like me. She still holds back sometimes, and I think she is the one who lets me know she's unhappy by getting physically sick, but we are working on a closer relationship.

266

I don't have a man in my life today. Someday, when I am healthier, I do want to have a relationship with someone who will respect and love me for who I am. Today, I am giving those things to myself. Until I learn to love me, no one will.

I pray that you make the choice to recover. You never need to give your life and power over to a sex addict again.

Love,

Marie

An Open Letter to Women Who Love Sex Addicts:

I never dreamed I would have something this valuable to share. I used to believe that I wasn't important because God had let so many bad things happen in my life. My husband was a sex addict, and he wanted not only other women, but other men too. He wanted me to participate with him in these sex excursions. I was totally ashamed of myself and him. Divorce was not an option. I was lost, and didn't know what to do.

Then I found Co-SA. The women in my group loved me right away, even when I was so sure I was unlovable. They helped me to see my part in the problems in my marriage. They showed me how to stand up for myself, and get help for me and my kids, no matter what my husband did.

Today my husband is in a recovery program. He has a sponsor, and I try not to pry into how his program is going. It's hard, because I still think I can control him if I try hard enough. It hurt so badly to have him out of control, and sometimes I let my fear of that happening again lead me back into checking up on him.

My sponsor and friends in Co-SA remind me that his program is none of my business. Just for today, I have chosen to try to work on this marriage. God willing, my husband will continue to recover, and we can be true partners again.

If there was just one thing I would tell you, it's that people can stay married and both get well. There is hope for sex addicts and co-sex addicts too.

Wishing recovery for your family,
Janine

(Author's Note: The following letter is from a woman who was raped at gunpoint by a man her family thought she should marry. She carried the pain of that incident around for over two years before coming to Co-SA meetings at the suggestion of her doctor.)

Dear Co-SA,

I will tell you what the women in the group told me: I believe you. You are not crazy. What you think happened did happen. If you have been abused, the people in Co-SA can help you find your hope and strength again. Please come.
Jennifer

Hello,

I am the mother of four children, all grown or nearly grown. Their father, my husband, is a recovering sex addict. I have been in Co-SA for over two years. In that time I have watched my children become involved with alcohol and drugs. I have watched one daughter have a baby out of wedlock, after going to chemical dependency treatment. I have watched the children learn the truth about their father's past behavior. And up until a few months ago, I kept my smiling face and tried to pretend I wasn't upset by all of it.

About three months ago, my anger welled up and hit me like a ton of bricks. I moved out of our bedroom, and told my husband we needed a divorce. I had learned more about his acting out. I realized that all along I had been denying my feelings about what he had done with our friends and our daughters' friends. Thank God my husband had a sponsor, and enough recovery to just let me have my feelings. He didn't tell me I shouldn't be angry with him. I was finally able to cry and yell and scream at him, at God, at myself for having stayed twenty-five years in this marriage.

The last three months have been a miracle for me. My daughter had her child, and, thanks to a miracle straight from heaven, will be able to keep the baby. My daughter is still working a program of her own for her alcoholism and drug addiction, and will soon be marrying a fine young man who is also in recovery. My husband and I are able to talk more intimately than we ever have before. My husband lost his job recently, but even that has not destroyed our new ability to be honest with each other.

I'm sure we will continue to grow. I don't know what the future will bring, but I do know that with the help of God and Co-SA, I will be able to handle it and to FEEL it.

Bless you,

Betty

Dear friends,

I wish I could express to you the warmth and caring I have experienced in recovery meetings. There is no way to really put it down on paper. Please go to a meeting and find some of that love and friendship for yourself today. You deserve it. You don't need to be confused and alone anymore.

Love,
Shari

Dear Friends,

I want to tell you about the hardest thing I've had to live through since being in Co-SA. Last summer, when I had three years in Co-SA and many more years in Al-Anon, I attended a family therapy session with my sixteen year old daughter, who had lived in a group home for two years after being treated for depression. Michelle and I had had our ups and downs, but overall our relationship seemed to be getting better. I wanted to believe that my recovery had made a difference in her life. I wanted to believe that the problems she was experiencing now were more due to her dad's untreated sexual addiction, even though she only spent summers and Christmases with him. I was not at all ready for the bomb she dropped that day.

With tears and sobs, she told me that she had been sexually abused by a teenage boy who was the son of a man I dated and lived with when she was 8 years old. I wept as she told me, "When you would go to Al-Anon meetings, Tommy would make me touch his penis. I never told you because I thought you wouldn't believe me, that you would rather have Jerry in your life, even if Tommy was abusing me."

It's very difficult to tell you how I felt. Physically, I was dizzy. I felt like I'd been hit by a truck. Emotionally, I was devastated. I had been so sure that if she'd been abused it had been by her father or someone in his family. I'd never taken her around the abusive men from my family.

Thanks to having worked a program all these years, I did not deny Michelle her truth. I know the devastation of childhood sexual abuse. I know how I felt, and still feel, when my mother tells me I should be over all that by now. I was able to give her the right to feel however she needs to feel. She was very adamant that she would seek her own recovery and find her own support group, and would decide by herself whether or not to confront this person who is now a young man.

I went straight from that therapy session to a meeting and talked about what was going on. I raged at this terrible disease that sets us up to be attracted to situations where we or our children can be abused. I cried, and the women there just sat with me while I felt the devastation of having placed my daughter in the kind of dangerous situation I'd grown up in. I almost cry just thinking about it now.

Michelle is still in therapy with a very kind, loving woman. She still lives at the group home, but we see each other often. She is beginning to come to me with questions about sexual abuse recovery. I am grateful that I have experience, strength, and hope to share with her, as she is ready to receive it. If I'd had a choice, I would have rather just shared recipes and shopping excursions with her, though.

Today I am married to a man who is not a sex addict. He is a recovering alcoholic who works a strong program of his own, and allows me to work mine. He has been a tremendous support to me through all the pain I've felt since Michelle's disclosure. He is a role model to her of what a healthy man can be. She is able to see my growth and healthier choices. I hope it will lead her to make healthier choices for her life.

Karen

Appendix A

The following list of feeling words has been designed for use with the Feelings Exercise in Chapter 20.

Abandoned	Amused	Attractive
Abused	Angry	Aware
Aching	Anguished	Awestruck
Accepted	Annoyed	Badgered
Accused	Anxious	Baited
Accepting	Apart	Bashful
Admired	Apathetic	Battered
Adored	Apologetic	Beaten
Adventurous	Appreciated	Beautiful
Affectionate	Appreciative	Belligerent
Agony	Apprehensive	Belittled
Alienated	Appropriate	Bereaved
Aloof	Approved	Betrayed
Aggravated	Argumentative	Bewildered
Agreeable	Aroused	Blamed
Aggressive	Astonished	Blaming
Alive	Assertive	Bonded
Alone	Attached	Bored
Alluring	Attacked	Bothered
Amazed	Attentive	Brave

Breathless	Competitive	Deceived
Bristling	Complacent	Deceptive
Broken-up	Complete	Defensive
Bruised	Confident	Delicate
Bubbly	Confused	Delighted
Burdened	Considerate	Demeaned
Burned	Consumed	Demoralized
Callous	Content	Dependent
Calm	Cool	Depressed
Capable	Courageous	Deprived
Captivated	Courteous	Deserted
Carefree	Coy	Desirable
Careful	Crabby	Desired
Careless	Cranky	Despair
Caring	Crazy	Despondent
Cautious	Creative	Destroyed
Certain	Critical	Different
Chased	Criticized	Dirty
Cheated	Cross	Disenchanted
Cheerful	Crushed	Disgusted
Childlike	Cuddly	Disinterested
Choked-up	Curious	Dispirited
Close	Cut	Distressed
Cold	Damned	Distrustful
Comfortable	Dangerous	Distrusted
Comforted	Daring	Disturbed
Competent	Dead	Dominated

Domineering
Doomed
Doubtful
Down
Dreadful
Eager
Ecstatic
Edgy
Edified
Elated
Embarrassed
Empowered
Empty
Enraged
Enraptured
Enthusiastic
Enticed
Esteemed
Exasperated
Excited
Exhilarated
Exposed
Fake
Fascinated
Feisty
Ferocious
Foolish

Forced
Forceful
Forgiven
Forgotten
Free
Friendly
Frightened
Frustrated
Full
Funny
Furious
Gay
Generous
Gentle
Genuine
Giddy
Giving
Goofy
Grateful
Greedy
Grief
Grim
Grimy
Grouchy
Grumpy
Hard
Harried

Hassled
Healthy
Helpful
Helpless
Hesitant
High
Hollow
Honest
Hopeful
Hopeless
Horrified
Hostile
Humiliated
Hurried
Hurt
Hyper
Ignorant
Ignored
Immature
Impatient
Important
Impotent
Impressed
Incompetent
Incomplete
Independent
Insecure

Innocent	Lustful	Panicked
Insignificant	Mad	Paralyzed
Insincere	Maudlin	Paranoid
Isolated	Malicious	Patient
Inspired	Mean	Peaceful
Insulted	Miserable	Pensive
Interested	Misunderstood	Perceptive
Intimate	Moody	Perturbed
Intolerant	Morose	Phony
Involved	Mournful	Pleasant
Irate	Mystified	Pleased
Irrational	Nasty	Positive
Irked	Nervous	Powerless
Irresponsible	Nice	Present
Irritable	Numb	Precious
Irritated	Nurtured	Pressured
Isolated	Nuts	Pretty
Jealous	Obsessed	Proud
Jittery	Offended	Pulled apart
Joyous	Open	Put down
Lively	Ornery	Puzzled
Lonely	Out of control	Quarrelsome
Loose	Overcome	Queer
Lost	Overjoyed	Quiet
Loving	Overpowered	Raped
Low	Overwhelmed	Ravished
Lucky	Pampered	Ravishing

Real	Satisfied	Soft
Refreshed	Scared	Solid
Regretful	Scolded	Solitary
Rejected	Scorned	Sorry
Rejuvenated	Scrutinized	Spacey
Rejecting	Secure	Special
Relaxed	Seduced	Spiteful
Relieved	Seductive	Spontaneous
Remarkable	Self-centered	Squelched
Remembered	Self-conscious	Starved
Removed	Selfish	Stiff
Repulsed	Separated	Stimulated
Repulsive	Sensuous	Stifled
Resentful	Sexy	Strangled
Resistant	Shattered	Strong
Responsible	Shocked	Stubborn
Responsive	Shot down	Stuck
Repressed	Shy	Stunned
Respected	Sickened	Stupid
Restless	Silly	Subdued
Revolted	Sincere	Submissive
Riled	Sinking	Successful
Rotten	Smart	Suffocated
Ruined	Smothered	Sure
Sad	Smug	Sweet
Safe	Sneaky	Sympathy
Satiated	Snowed	Tainted

Tearful	Uncomfortable	Wary
Tender	Under control	Weak
Tense	Understanding	Whipped
Terrific	Understood	Whole
Terrified	Undesirable	Wicked
Thrilled	Unfriendly	Wild
Ticked	Ungrateful	Willing
Tickled	Unified	Wiped out
Tight	Unhappy	Wishful
Timid	Unimpressed	Withdrawn
Tired	Unsafe	Wonderful
Tolerant	Unstable	Worried
Tormented	Upset	Worthy
Torn	Uptight	Wounded
Tortured	Used	Young
Touched	Useful	Zapped
Trapped	Useless	
Tremendous	Unworthy	
Tricked	Validated	
Trusted	Valuable	
Trustful	Valued	
Trusting	Victorious	
Ugly	Violated	
Unacceptable	Violent	
Unapproachable	Voluptuous	
Unaware	Vulnerable	
Uncertain	Warm	

Appendix B
Helpful Numbers

Co-SA Minnesota
P. O. Box 14537
Minneapolis, MN   55414
(612) 537-6904

Sex and Love Addicts Anonymous
Fellowship Wide Services Inc. (SLAA)
P. O. Box 119
Newtown Branch
Boston, MA   02258
(617) 332-1845

Sex Addicts Anonymous
No address available
(612) 339-0217

Sexaholics Anonymous
No address available
(612) 898-8017

Del Amo Hospital
23700 Camino Del Sol
Florence, CA   90505
Crisis Line
1-800-551-9888

Your local Council
on Alcoholism and
Drug Abuse may have
listings for
meetings in your
community.

Also check the white
pages of your phone
book.

Psychiatric and Drug
Treatment hospitals
frequently have
meeting times and
dates available.

More Books From
Discovery Press
1-800-775-8865

Item	Quan.	Price	Total
Women Who Love Sex Addicts	____	x $12.95	_____
Steps 1-5 Workbook for Co-Sex Addict's	____	x $8.95	_____
Steps 1-5 Workbook for Sex Addicts	____	x $8.95	_____
Steps 1-5 Workbook for Alcohol/Drug Addiction *for Adults*	____	x $8.95	_____
Steps 1-5 Workbook for Alcohol/Drug Addiction *for Young Adults*	____	x $8.95	_____

Sub Total _____

7.75% Sales Tax in Texas _____

Add $1.40 Shipping and $.50 for each additional book _____

Please allow 4-6 weeks delivery **TOTAL** _____

To order call 1-800-775-8865 or (817) 732-8780

VISA # _____ Exp. Date _____

Name _____ Signature _____

Address _____

State _____ Zip _____

Or mail to: Discovery Press
6500 West Freeway, Suite 202 • Ft. Worth, TX 76116
FAX 817-732-8929